God Says:

I am so proud of you. As you write, remember my love for you. Remember that I have magnified my word, above all, my name. Remember that what I speak out of my mouth will not return to me void. Trust that you <u>can</u> hear from me..trust in that still small voice—remember, my thoughts are not your thoughts. Trust me when I tell you I love you and I'm proud of you. Trust me when I give a word of warning and trust me when I give you a word of rebuke. In my word, I remind you that I reveal my secrets and share my covenant with those who revere me. Use this journal as an opportunity to walk closely with me, allow me to train your thoughts and renew your mind. Let me regulate your emotions, and let me teach you how to test every spirit. In all things, trust that my heart for you will never change. You will always be the apple of my eye, my royal priesthood, a true king's kid. No longer should you call me master; call me, "friend" and I will call you beloved.

Love, God

Pray this prayer as often as you feel led before writing in this journal:

God, I bind up the spirit of deception. As I write to you and your Holy Spirit writes through me, I will only hear from the voice of God. I decree you are my shepherd and I will hear you, only. Help me to learn your voice. Tune my ears to your frequency. Teach me how to test every spirit and align your voice with your written word. Selah.

"And blessed is she that believed: for there shall be a performance [fulfillment] of those things which were told her from the Lord. Luke 1:45 KJV

God Says: _____/_____/_____

_____

_____

_____

_____

_____

_____

_____

_____

_____

_____

_____

_____

_____

_____

_____

_____

_____

"that if you confess with your mouth the Lord Jesus and believe in your heart that God has raised Him from the dead, you will be saved. For with the heart one believes unto righteousness, and with the mouth confession is made unto salvation." Romans 10:9-10 NKJV

God Says: _____ / _____ / _____

_____

_____

_____

_____

_____

_____

_____

_____

_____

_____

_____

_____

_____

_____

_____

_____

_____

"This is Jacob, the generation of those who seek Him, Who seek Your face. *Selah*"
Psalms 24:6 NKJV

God Says: _____/_____/_____

_____

_____

_____

_____

_____

_____

_____

_____

_____

_____

_____

_____

_____

_____

_____

_____

_____

_____

_____

"As the deer pants for the water brooks, So pants my soul for You, O God."
Psalms 42:1 NKJV

God Says: _____/_____/_____

_____

_____

_____

_____

_____

_____

_____

_____

_____

_____

_____

_____

_____

_____

_____

_____

_____

_____

"Rest in the Lord, and wait patiently for Him; Do not fret because of him who prospers in his way, Because of the man who brings wicked schemes to pass." Psalms 37:7 NKJV

God Says: ____/____/____

_____

_____

_____

_____

_____

_____

_____

_____

_____

_____

_____

_____

_____

_____

_____

_____

_____

"God is our refuge and strength, A very present help in trouble."
Psalms 46:1 KJV

God Says:

_____ / _____ / _____

_____

_____

_____

_____

_____

_____

_____

_____

_____

_____

_____

_____

_____

_____

_____

_____

_____

_____

_____

_____

_____

"Deep calleth unto deep at the noise of thy waterfalls: All thy waves and thy billows are gone over me." Psalms 42:7 ASV

God Says: _____/_____/_____

_____

_____

_____

_____

_____

_____

_____

_____

_____

_____

_____

_____

_____

_____

_____

_____

_____

"Preach the word! Be ready in season and out of season. Convince, rebuke, exhort, with all long-suffering and teaching." II Timothy 4:2 NKJV

God Says: _____ / _____ / _____

_____

_____

_____

_____

_____

_____

_____

_____

_____

_____

_____

_____

_____

_____

_____

_____

_____

_____

"Bless the Lord, O my soul, And forget not all His benefits:" Psalms 103:2 KJV

God Says: _____/_____/_____

_____

_____

_____

_____

_____

_____

_____

_____

_____

_____

_____

_____

_____

_____

_____

_____

_____

_____

"I thank my God always, making mention of thee in my prayers,"
Philemon 1:4 ASV

God Says: ____ / ____ / ____

_____

_____

_____

_____

_____

_____

_____

_____

_____

_____

_____

_____

_____

_____

_____

_____

_____

_____

"Therefore by their fruits ye shall know them."
Matthew 7:20 ASV

God Says: _____/_____/_____

_____

_____

_____

_____

_____

_____

_____

_____

_____

_____

_____

_____

_____

_____

_____

_____

_____

_____

"The blessing of the LORD, it maketh rich, And He addeth no sorrow with it."
Proverbs 10:22 KJV

God Says: _____/_____/_____

_____

_____

_____

_____

_____

_____

_____

_____

_____

_____

_____

_____

_____

_____

_____

_____

_____

_____

"Before the year was out, Hannah had conceived and given birth to a son. She named him Samuel, explaining, "I asked God for him."" 1 Samuel 1:20 MSG

God Says: _____/_____/_____

_____

_____

_____

_____

_____

_____

_____

_____

_____

_____

_____

_____

_____

_____

_____

_____

_____

_____

_____

"You crown the year with Your goodness, And Your paths drip with abundance."
Psalms 65:11 NKJV

God Says: _____/_____/_____

_____

_____

_____

_____

_____

_____

_____

_____

_____

_____

_____

_____

_____

_____

_____

_____

_____

_____

_____

_____

"Be not deceived; God is not mocked: for whatsoever a man soweth, that shall he also reap."
Galatians 6:7 KJV

God Says: _____/_____/_____

_____

_____

_____

_____

_____

_____

_____

_____

_____

_____

_____

_____

_____

_____

_____

_____

_____

"I wait for the Lord, my soul waits, And in His word I do hope."
Psalms 130:5 NKJV

God Says: _____/_____/_____

_____

_____

_____

_____

_____

_____

_____

_____

_____

_____

_____

_____

_____

_____

_____

_____

_____

_____

_____

_____

"Mercy, peace, and love be multiplied to you."
Jude 1:2 NKJV

God Says: _____/_____/_____

_____

_____

_____

_____

_____

_____

_____

_____

_____

_____

_____

_____

_____

_____

_____

_____

_____

_____

_____

"For I reckon that the sufferings of this present time are not worthy to be compared with the
glory which shall be revealed in us."
Romans 8:18 KJV

God Says: _____ / _____ / _____

_____

_____

_____

_____

_____

_____

_____

_____

_____

_____

_____

_____

_____

_____

_____

_____

_____

_____

_____

_____

_____

"Discretion shall preserve thee, Understanding shall keep thee," Proverbs 2:11 KJV

God Says: _____/_____/_____

_____

_____

_____

_____

_____

_____

_____

_____

_____

_____

_____

_____

_____

_____

_____

_____

_____

_____

"How can I curse those whom God has not cursed? How can I denounce those whom the Lord has not denounced?" Numbers 23:8 NIV

God Says: _____/_____/_____

_____

_____

_____

_____

_____

_____

_____

_____

_____

_____

_____

_____

_____

_____

_____

_____

_____

_____

_____

_____

"And he believed in the LORD; and he counted it to him for righteousness."
Genesis 15:6 KJV

God Says: _____/_____/_____

_____

_____

_____

_____

_____

_____

_____

_____

_____

_____

_____

_____

_____

_____

_____

_____

_____

_____

"May He grant you according to your heart's desire, And fulfill all your purpose."
Psalms 20:4 NKJV

God Says: _____/_____/_____

_____

_____

_____

_____

_____

_____

_____

_____

_____

_____

_____

_____

_____

_____

_____

_____

_____

_____

_____

_____

_____

"There failed not ought of any good thing which the LORD had spoken unto the house of Israel;
all came to pass."Joshua 21:45 KJV

God Says: _____/_____/_____

_____

_____

_____

_____

_____

_____

_____

_____

_____

_____

_____

_____

_____

_____

_____

_____

_____

_____

_____

"I will break down your stubborn pride and make the sky above you like iron and the ground beneath you like bronze." Leviticus 26:19 NIV

God Says: _____/_____/_____

_____

_____

_____

_____

_____

_____

_____

_____

_____

_____

_____

_____

_____

_____

_____

_____

_____

_____

"There is no peace, saith the LORD, unto the wicked."
Isaiah 48:22 KJV

God Says: _____/_____/_____

_____

_____

_____

_____

_____

_____

_____

_____

_____

_____

_____

_____

_____

_____

_____

_____

_____

"We are hard pressed on every side, but not crushed; perplexed, but not in despair; persecuted, but not abandoned; struck down, but not destroyed."
2 Corinthians 4:8-9 NIV

God Says: _____ / _____ / _____

_____

_____

_____

_____

_____

_____

_____

_____

_____

_____

_____

_____

_____

_____

_____

_____

"For ye shall go out with joy, and be led forth with peace: the mountains and the hills shall break forth before you into singing; and all the trees of the fields shall clap their hands."
Isaiah 55:12 ASV

God Says: _____/_____/_____

_____

_____

_____

_____

_____

_____

_____

_____

_____

_____

_____

_____

_____

_____

_____

_____

_____

_____

"A brother offended is harder to be won than a strong city; And such contentions are like the bars of a castle." Proverbs 18:19 ASV

God Says: _____/_____/_____

_____

_____

_____

_____

_____

_____

_____

_____

_____

_____

_____

_____

_____

_____

_____

_____

_____

_____

"But the Lord said to Samuel, "Do not look at his appearance or at his physical stature, because I have refused him. For the Lord does not see as man sees; for man looks at the outward appearance, but the Lord looks at the heart."" I Samuel 16:7 NKJV

God Says: _____/_____/_____

_____

_____

_____

_____

_____

_____

_____

_____

_____

_____

_____

_____

_____

_____

_____

_____

_____

_____

_____

"For to be carnally minded is death; but to be spiritually minded is life and peace. Because the carnal mind is enmity against God: for it is not subject to the law of God, neither indeed can be."
Romans 8:6-7 KJV

God Says: _____/_____/_____

_____

_____

_____

_____

_____

_____

_____

_____

_____

_____

_____

_____

_____

_____

_____

_____

_____

_____

_____

"But upon mount Zion shall be deliverance, and there shall be holiness; and the house of Jacob
shall possess their possessions."
Obadiah 1:17 KJV

God Says: _____/_____/_____

_____

_____

_____

_____

_____

_____

_____

_____

_____

_____

_____

_____

_____

_____

_____

_____

_____

_____

_____

"The LORD shall fight for you, and ye shall hold your peace."
Exodus 14:14 KJV

God Says: _____ / _____ / _____

_____

_____

_____

_____

_____

_____

_____

_____

_____

_____

_____

_____

_____

_____

_____

_____

_____

_____

"The Lord said to me, "You have seen correctly, for I am watching to see that my word is fulfilled."" Jeremiah 1:12 NIV

God Says: _____/_____/_____

_____

_____

_____

_____

_____

_____

_____

_____

_____

_____

_____

_____

_____

_____

_____

_____

_____

"So David inquired of the Lord, saying, "Shall I pursue this troop? Shall I overtake them?" And
He answered him, "Pursue, for you shall surely overtake them and without fail recover all.""
I Samuel 30:8 NKJV

God Says: _____/_____/_____

_____

_____

_____

_____

_____

_____

_____

_____

_____

_____

_____

_____

_____

_____

_____

_____

_____

_____

_____

_____

"The sacrifice pleasing to God is a broken spirit. God, You will not despise a broken and humbled heart." Psalms 51:17 HCSB

God Says: _____/_____/_____

_____

_____

_____

_____

_____

_____

_____

_____

_____

_____

_____

_____

_____

_____

_____

_____

_____

_____

_____

"You shall dwell in the land of Goshen, and you shall be near to me, you and your children, your children's children, your flocks and your herds, and all that you have." Genesis 45:10 NKJV

God Says: _____/_____/_____

_____

_____

_____

_____

_____

_____

_____

_____

_____

_____

_____

_____

_____

_____

_____

_____

_____

_____

"Is not my word like fire," declares the LORD, "and like a hammer that breaks a rock in pieces?""
Jeremiah 23:29 NIV

God Says: _____/_____/_____

_____

_____

_____

_____

_____

_____

_____

_____

_____

_____

_____

_____

_____

_____

_____

_____

_____

_____

_____

""At that time"—this is God's Message still— "you'll address me, 'Dear husband!' Never again will you address me, 'My slave-master!'"" Hosea 2:16 MSG

God Says: _____/_____/_____

_____

_____

_____

_____

_____

_____

_____

_____

_____

_____

_____

_____

_____

_____

_____

_____

_____

_____

"No weapon that is formed against thee shall prosper; and every tongue that shall rise against thee in judgment thou shalt condemn. This is the heritage of the servants of the LORD, and their righteousness is of me, saith the LORD." Isaiah 54:17 KJV

God Says: _____/_____/_____

_____

_____

_____

_____

_____

_____

_____

_____

_____

_____

_____

_____

_____

_____

_____

_____

_____

_____

_____

"Do not fear, nor be afraid; Have I not told you from that time, and declared it? You are My witnesses. Is there a God besides Me? Indeed there is no other Rock; I know not one."
Isaiah 44:8 NKJV

God Says: _____/_____/_____

"How precious also are thy thoughts unto me, O God! How great is the sum of them! If I should count them, they are more in number than the sand: When I awake, I am still with thee."
Psalm 139:17-18 KJV

God Says:

_____ / _____ / _____

_____

_____

_____

_____

_____

_____

_____

_____

_____

_____

_____

_____

_____

_____

_____

_____

_____

"When the Spirit of truth comes, he will guide you into all truth. He will not speak on his own but will tell you what he has heard. He will tell you about the future."

John 16:13 NLT

God Says: ____ / ____ / ____

_____

_____

_____

_____

_____

_____

_____

_____

_____

_____

_____

_____

_____

_____

_____

_____

_____

_____

_____

"Looking up to heaven, he sighed and said, "Ephphatha," which means, "Be opened!""
Mark 7:34 NLT

God Says: _____/_____/_____

_____

_____

_____

_____

_____

_____

_____

_____

_____

_____

_____

_____

_____

_____

_____

_____

"He fills my life with good things. My youth is renewed like the eagle's!"
Psalms 103:5 NLT

God Says: ____/____/____

_____

_____

_____

_____

_____

_____

_____

_____

_____

_____

_____

_____

_____

_____

_____

_____

_____

_____

_____

_____

"Behold, they shall surely gather together, but not by me: whosoever shall gather together against thee shall fall for thy sake."
Isaiah 54:15 KJV

God Says:

_____/_____/_____

_____

_____

_____

_____

_____

_____

_____

_____

_____

_____

_____

_____

_____

_____

_____

_____

_____

_____

_____

"Remember, it is sin to know what you ought to do and then not do it."
James 4:17 NLT

God Says: _____ / _____ / _____

_____

_____

_____

_____

_____

_____

_____

_____

_____

_____

_____

_____

_____

_____

_____

_____

_____

_____

_____

_____

_____

"The Lord will conquer your enemies when they attack you. They will attack you from one direction, but they will scatter from you in seven!"
Deuteronomy 28:7 NLT

God Says: _____ / _____ / _____

_____

_____

_____

_____

_____

_____

_____

_____

_____

_____

_____

_____

_____

_____

_____

_____

_____

"You will not have to fight this battle. Take up your positions; stand firm and see the deliverance the Lord will give you, Judah and Jerusalem. Do not be afraid; do not be discouraged. Go out to face them tomorrow, and the Lord will be with you."

2 Chronicles 20:17 NIV

God Says: _____ / _____ / _____

_____

_____

_____

_____

_____

_____

_____

_____

_____

_____

_____

_____

_____

_____

_____

_____

_____

_____

_____

"The Lord of Hosts Himself has planned it; therefore, who can stand in its way? It is His hand that is outstretched, so who can turn it back?"
Isaiah 14:27 HCSB

God Says: _____/_____/_____

_____

_____

_____

_____

_____

_____

_____

_____

_____

_____

_____

_____

_____

_____

_____

_____

_____

_____

"Shall two walk together, except they have agreed?"
Amos 3:3 ASV

God Says: _____ / _____ / _____

_____

_____

_____

_____

_____

_____

_____

_____

_____

_____

_____

_____

_____

_____

_____

_____

_____

_____

"They that sow in tears shall reap in joy." Psalms 126:5 ASV

God Says: _____/_____/_____

_____

_____

_____

_____

_____

_____

_____

_____

_____

_____

_____

_____

_____

_____

_____

_____

_____

_____

_____

"Isaac sowed seed in that land, and in that year he reaped a hundred times what was sown. The Lord blessed him," Genesis 26:12 HCSB

God Says: _____/_____/_____

_____

_____

_____

_____

_____

_____

_____

_____

_____

_____

_____

_____

_____

_____

_____

_____

_____

_____

"Then he continued, "Do not be afraid, Daniel. Since the first day that you set your mind to gain understanding and to humble yourself before your God, your words were heard, and I have come in response to them."" Daniel 10:12 NIV

God Says: _____/_____/_____

_____

_____

_____

_____

_____

_____

_____

_____

_____

_____

_____

_____

_____

_____

_____

_____

_____

_____

_____

"A thief comes only to steal and to kill and to destroy. I have come so that they may have life and have it in abundance." John 10:10 HCSB

God Says:

_____ / _____ / _____

_____

_____

_____

_____

_____

_____

_____

_____

_____

_____

_____

_____

_____

_____

_____

_____

_____

_____

"Cast your cares on the Lord and he will sustain you; he will never let the righteous be shaken."
Psalms 55:22 NIV

God Says:

_____ / _____ / _____

_____

_____

_____

_____

_____

_____

_____

_____

_____

_____

_____

_____

_____

_____

_____

_____

_____

_____

"And it shall come to pass that, before they call, I will answer; and while they are yet speaking, I will hear." Isaiah 65:24 ASV

God Says: _____/_____/_____

_____

_____

_____

_____

_____

_____

_____

_____

_____

_____

_____

_____

_____

_____

_____

_____

_____

_____

_____

"Before he had finished praying, Rebekah came out with her jar on her shoulder. She was the daughter of Bethuel son of Milkah, who was the wife of Abraham's brother Nahor."
Genesis 24:15 NIV

God Says: _____/_____/_____

_____

_____

_____

_____

_____

_____

_____

_____

_____

_____

_____

_____

_____

_____

_____

_____

_____

"The LORD is on my side; I will not fear: What can man do unto me? It is better to trust in the LORD Than to put confidence in man. It is better to trust in the LORD Than to put confidence in princes." Psalm 118:6, 8-9 KJV

God Says:

_____/_____/_____

"My covenant will I not break, Nor alter the thing that is gone out of my lips."

Psalms 89:34 ASV

God Says: _____/_____/_____

_____

_____

_____

_____

_____

_____

_____

_____

_____

_____

_____

_____

_____

_____

_____

_____

_____

_____

_____

_____

"For if you remain silent at this time, relief and deliverance for the Jews will arise from another place, but you and your father's family will perish. And who knows but that you have come to your royal position for such a time as this?" Esther 4:14 NIV

God Says: _____/_____/_____

_____

_____

_____

_____

_____

_____

_____

_____

_____

_____

_____

_____

_____

_____

_____

_____

_____

_____

""For the mountains may move and the hills disappear, but even then my faithful love for you will remain. My covenant of blessing will never be broken," says the Lord, who has mercy on you." Isaiah 54:10 NLT

God Says: _____/_____/_____

_____

_____

_____

_____

_____

_____

_____

_____

_____

_____

_____

_____

_____

_____

_____

_____

_____

_____

"For he is our peace, who hath made both one, and hath broken down the middle wall of partition between us;" Ephesians 2:14 KJV

God Says: _____/_____/_____

_____

_____

_____

_____

_____

_____

_____

_____

_____

_____

_____

_____

_____

_____

_____

_____

_____

_____

"But let patience have her perfect work, that ye may be perfect and entire, wanting nothing."
James 1:4 KJV

God Says: _____ / _____ / _____

_____

_____

_____

_____

_____

_____

_____

_____

_____

_____

_____

_____

_____

_____

_____

_____

_____

_____

"I would have lost heart, unless I had believed That I would see the goodness of the Lord In the land of the living. Wait on the Lord; Be of good courage, And He shall strengthen your heart; Wait, I say, on the Lord!" Psalms 27:13-14 NKJV

God Says: _____/_____/_____

_____

_____

_____

_____

_____

_____

_____

_____

_____

_____

_____

_____

_____

_____

_____

_____

_____

_____

_____

_____

_____

"May the God of hope fill you with all joy and all peace as you trust in him, so that you may overflow with hope by the power of the Holy Spirit." Romans 15:13 NIV

God Says:

_____/_____/_____

"Instead of your shame you shall have double honor, And instead of confusion they shall rejoice in their portion. Therefore in their land they shall possess double; Everlasting joy shall be theirs."

Isaiah 61:7 NKJV

God Says:

_____ / _____ / _____

"For I, saith the LORD, will be unto her a wall of fire round about, and will be the glory in the midst of her." Zechariah 2:5 KJV

God Says: _____/_____/_____

_____

_____

_____

_____

_____

_____

_____

_____

_____

_____

_____

_____

_____

_____

_____

_____

_____

_____

"Before destruction the heart of man is haughty, And before honour is humility."
Proverbs 18:12 KJV

God Says: _____/_____/_____

_____

_____

_____

_____

_____

_____

_____

_____

_____

_____

_____

_____

_____

_____

_____

_____

_____

_____

"For this child I prayed; and the LORD hath given me my petition which I asked of him:"
1 Samuel 1:27 KJV

God Says: _____/_____/_____

_____

_____

_____

_____

_____

_____

_____

_____

_____

_____

_____

_____

_____

_____

_____

_____

_____

_____

"Every good and perfect gift is from above, coming down from the Father of the heavenly lights, who does not change like shifting shadows." James 1:17 NIV

God Says: _____/_____/_____

_____

_____

_____

_____

_____

_____

_____

_____

_____

_____

_____

_____

_____

_____

_____

_____

"If it had not been the LORD who was on our side, now may Israel say; If it had not been the LORD who was on our side, when men rose up against us:"

Psalm 124:1-2 KJV

God Says: _____/_____/_____

_____

_____

_____

_____

_____

_____

_____

_____

_____

_____

_____

_____

_____

_____

_____

_____

_____

_____

_____

"You ask and do not receive, because you ask amiss, that you may spend it on your pleasures."
James 4:3 NKJV

God Says: _____/_____/_____

_____

_____

_____

_____

_____

_____

_____

_____

_____

_____

_____

_____

_____

_____

_____

_____

_____

"This day I call the heavens and the earth as witnesses against you that I have set before you life and death, blessings and curses. Now choose life, so that you and your children may live"
Deuteronomy 30:19 NIV

God Says: _____/_____/_____

_____

_____

_____

_____

_____

_____

_____

_____

_____

_____

_____

_____

_____

_____

_____

_____

_____

_____

_____

"He has made everything beautiful in its time. He has also set eternity in the human heart; yet no
one can fathom what God has done from beginning to end."
Ecclesiastes 3:11 NIV

God Says: _____/_____/_____

_____

_____

_____

_____

_____

_____

_____

_____

_____

_____

_____

_____

_____

_____

_____

_____

_____

_____

_____

_____

_____

"Whoever dwells in the shelter of the Most High will rest in the shadow of the Almighty."
Psalms 91:1 NIV

God Says: _____/_____/_____

_____

_____

_____

_____

_____

_____

_____

_____

_____

_____

_____

_____

_____

_____

_____

_____

_____

_____

"The time is coming when everything that is covered up will be revealed, and all that is secret will be made known to all. Whatever you have said in the dark will be heard in the light, and what you have whispered behind closed doors will be shouted from the housetops for all to hear!" Luke 12:2-3 NLT

God Says: _____/_____/_____

_____

_____

_____

_____

_____

_____

_____

_____

_____

_____

_____

_____

_____

_____

_____

_____

_____

_____

_____

_____

"And I, if I am lifted up from the earth, will draw all men unto me."
John 12:32 KJV

God Says: _____/_____/_____

_____

_____

_____

_____

_____

_____

_____

_____

_____

_____

_____

_____

_____

_____

_____

_____

_____

_____

_____

_____

"For the word of God is living and effective and sharper than any double-edged sword, penetrating as far as the separation of soul and spirit, joints and marrow. It is able to judge the ideas and thoughts of the heart." Hebrews 4:12 HCSB

God Says: _____ / _____ / _____

_____

_____

_____

_____

_____

_____

_____

_____

_____

_____

_____

_____

_____

_____

_____

_____

_____

_____

_____

"Again he said unto me, Prophesy upon these bones, and say unto them, O ye dry bones, hear the word of the LORD." Ezekiel 37:4 KJV

God Says: 　　　　　＿＿＿＿/＿＿＿＿/＿＿＿＿

_____

_____

_____

_____

_____

_____

_____

_____

_____

_____

_____

_____

_____

_____

_____

_____

_____

_____

"Only with thine eyes shalt thou behold And see the reward of the wicked."
Psalm 91:8 KJV

God Says: _____/_____/_____

_____

_____

_____

_____

_____

_____

_____

_____

_____

_____

_____

_____

_____

_____

_____

_____

_____

_____

"If you ignore criticism, you will end in poverty and disgrace; if you accept correction, you will be honored." Proverbs 13:18 NLT

God Says: _____ / _____ / _____

_____

_____

_____

_____

_____

_____

_____

_____

_____

_____

_____

_____

_____

_____

_____

_____

_____

_____

_____

"Cry aloud, spare not, lift up thy voice like a trumpet, and declare unto my people their transgression, and to the house of Jacob their sins."
Isaiah 58:1 ASV

God Says: _____/_____/_____

_____

_____

_____

_____

_____

_____

_____

_____

_____

_____

_____

_____

_____

_____

_____

_____

_____

"The king's heart is like a stream of water directed by the Lord; he guides it wherever he pleases." Proverbs 21:1 NLT

God Says: _____/_____/_____

_____

_____

_____

_____

_____

_____

_____

_____

_____

_____

_____

_____

_____

_____

_____

_____

_____

"And they that shall be of thee shall build the old waste places: thou shalt raise up the foundations of many generations; and thou shalt be called, The repairer of the breach, The restorer of paths to dwell in." Isaiah 58:12 KJV

God Says: _____ / _____ / _____

_____

_____

_____

_____

_____

_____

_____

_____

_____

_____

_____

_____

_____

_____

_____

_____

_____

_____

_____

_____

"Do not banish me from Your presence or take Your Holy Spirit from me."
Psalms 51:11 HCSB

God Says: _____/_____/_____

_____

_____

_____

_____

_____

_____

_____

_____

_____

_____

_____

_____

_____

_____

_____

_____

_____

"Surely goodness and mercy shall follow me All the days of my life; And I will dwell in the house of the Lord Forever." Psalms 23:6 NKJV

God Says: _____/_____/_____

_____

_____

_____

_____

_____

_____

_____

_____

_____

_____

_____

_____

_____

_____

_____

_____

_____

_____

_____

_____

"He looked up to heaven and with a deep sigh said to him, "Ephphatha!" (which means "Be opened!")." Mark 7:34 NIV

God Says: ____/____/____

_____

_____

_____

_____

_____

_____

_____

_____

_____

_____

_____

_____

_____

_____

_____

_____

_____

"For thy Maker is thine husband; the LORD of hosts is his name; and thy Redeemer the Holy
One of Israel; The God of the whole earth shall he be called."
Isaiah 54:5 KJV

God Says: _____/_____/_____

_____

_____

_____

_____

_____

_____

_____

_____

_____

_____

_____

_____

_____

_____

_____

_____

_____

"Then the angel of God, who had been leading the people of Israel, moved to the rear of the camp. The pillar of cloud also moved from the front and stood behind them."
Exodus 14:19 NLT

God Says: _____/_____/_____

_____

_____

_____

_____

_____

_____

_____

_____

_____

_____

_____

_____

_____

_____

_____

_____

_____

_____

"Thus says the Lord, your Redeemer, The Holy One of Israel: "I am the Lord your God, Who teaches you to profit, Who leads you by the way you should go."
Isaiah 48:17 NKJV

God Says: _____ / _____ / _____

_____

_____

_____

_____

_____

_____

_____

_____

_____

_____

_____

_____

_____

_____

_____

_____

_____

_____

_____

_____

"Thou shalt also decree a thing, and it shall be established unto thee: And the light shall shine upon thy ways." Job 22:28 KJV

God Says: _____/_____/_____

_____

_____

_____

_____

_____

_____

_____

_____

_____

_____

_____

_____

_____

_____

_____

_____

_____

_____

"Search me, God, and know my heart; test me and know my anxious thoughts. See if there is any offensive way in me, and lead me in the way everlasting."
Psalms 139:23-24 NIV

God Says:

_____/_____/_____

_____

_____

_____

_____

_____

_____

_____

_____

_____

_____

_____

_____

_____

_____

_____

_____

_____

_____

_____

"Dear friends, you always followed my instructions when I was with you. And now that I am away, it is even more important. Work hard to show the results of your salvation, obeying God with deep reverence and fear. For God is working in you, giving you the desire and the power to do what pleases him."
Philippians 2:12-13 NLT

God Says: _____ / _____ / _____

_____

_____

_____

_____

_____

_____

_____

_____

_____

_____

_____

_____

_____

_____

_____

_____

_____

_____

_____

"Watch that you don't treat a single one of these childlike believers arrogantly. You realize, don't you, that their personal angels are constantly in touch with my Father in heaven?"
Matthew 18:10 MSG

God Says: _____ / _____ / _____

_____

_____

_____

_____

_____

_____

_____

_____

_____

_____

_____

_____

_____

_____

_____

_____

_____

_____

_____

_____

_____

_____

"I, even I, am He who blots out your transgressions for My own sake; And I will not remember your sins. Put Me in remembrance; Let us contend together; State your case, that you may be acquitted." Isaiah 43:25-26 NKJV

God Says: _____/_____/_____

_____

_____

_____

_____

_____

_____

_____

_____

_____

_____

_____

_____

_____

_____

_____

_____

_____

_____

"A double minded man is unstable in all his ways."
James 1:8 KJV

God Says: ____/____/____

_____

_____

_____

_____

_____

_____

_____

_____

_____

_____

_____

_____

_____

_____

_____

_____

_____

_____

"You will not fear the terror of night, nor the arrow that flies by day, nor the pestilence that stalks in the darkness, nor the plague that destroys at midday."

Psalms 91:5-6 NIV

God Says: _____/_____/_____

_____

_____

_____

_____

_____

_____

_____

_____

_____

_____

_____

_____

_____

_____

_____

_____

_____

_____

"Be not afraid of their faces: for I am with thee to deliver thee, saith the LORD. Then the LORD put forth his hand, and touched my mouth. And the LORD said unto me, Behold, I have put my words in thy mouth." Jeremiah 1:8-9 KJV

God Says: 　　　　＿＿＿／＿＿＿／＿＿＿

_____

_____

_____

_____

_____

_____

_____

_____

_____

_____

_____

_____

_____

_____

_____

_____

_____

_____

_____

"And God said, Let there be light: and there was light."
Genesis 1:3 KJV

God Says: _____/_____/_____

_____

_____

_____

_____

_____

_____

_____

_____

_____

_____

_____

_____

_____

_____

_____

_____

_____

""Honor your father and mother." This is the first commandment with a promise: If you honor your father and mother, "things will go well for you, and you will have a long life on the earth.""

Ephesians 6:2-3 NLT

God Says: _____ / _____ / _____

_____

_____

_____

_____

_____

_____

_____

_____

_____

_____

_____

_____

_____

_____

_____

_____

_____

_____

"The course of my life is in Your power; deliver me from the power of my enemies and from my persecutors." Psalms 31:15 HCSB

God Says: _____/_____/_____

_____

_____

_____

_____

_____

_____

_____

_____

_____

_____

_____

_____

_____

_____

_____

_____

_____

_____

_____

_____

"Answer me quickly, Lord; my spirit fails. Do not hide your face from me or I will be like those who go down to the pit." Psalms 143:7 NIV

God Says: _____/_____/_____

_____

_____

_____

_____

_____

_____

_____

_____

_____

_____

_____

_____

_____

_____

_____

_____

_____

_____

"Behold, I send you out as sheep in the midst of wolves. Therefore be wise as serpents and harmless as doves." Matthew 10:16 NKJV

God Says: _____/_____/_____

_____

_____

_____

_____

_____

_____

_____

_____

_____

_____

_____

_____

_____

_____

_____

_____

_____

"Teach me to do Your will, For You are my God; Your Spirit is good. Lead me in the land of uprightness.
Revive me, O Lord, for Your name's sake! For Your righteousness' sake bring my soul out of trouble. In
Your mercy cut off my enemies, And destroy all those who afflict my soul; For I am Your servant."
Psalms 143:10-12 NKJV

God Says: ___/___/___

_____

_____

_____

_____

_____

_____

_____

_____

_____

_____

_____

_____

_____

_____

_____

_____

_____

_____

_____

_____

"Therefore prophesy against them, prophesy, O son of man."
Ezekiel 11:4 KJV

God Says: _____/_____/_____

_____

_____

_____

_____

_____

_____

_____

_____

_____

_____

_____

_____

_____

_____

_____

_____

_____

_____

"The steps of a good man are ordered by the LORD: And he delighteth in his way."
Psalm 37:23 KJV

God Says: _____/_____/_____

_____

_____

_____

_____

_____

_____

_____

_____

_____

_____

_____

_____

_____

_____

_____

_____

_____

_____

"Blessed is the man that endureth temptation: for when he is tried, he shall receive the crown of life, which the Lord hath promised to them that love him." James 1:12 KJV

God Says: _____/_____/_____

_____

_____

_____

_____

_____

_____

_____

_____

_____

_____

_____

_____

_____

_____

_____

_____

_____

_____

"Remember this: Whoever sows sparingly will also reap sparingly, and whoever sows generously will also reap generously." 2 Corinthians 9:6 NIV

God Says: _____ / _____ / _____

_____

_____

_____

_____

_____

_____

_____

_____

_____

_____

_____

_____

_____

_____

_____

_____

_____

_____

_____

"The LORD is my shepherd; I shall not want."
Psalms 23:1 KJV

God Says: _____/_____/_____

_____

_____

_____

_____

_____

_____

_____

_____

_____

_____

_____

_____

_____

_____

_____

_____

_____

_____

_____

_____

_____

"The LORD will perfect that which concerneth me: Thy mercy, O LORD, endureth for ever:
Forsake not the works of thine own hands." Psalm 138:8 KJV

God Says: _____ / _____ / _____

_____

_____

_____

_____

_____

_____

_____

_____

_____

_____

_____

_____

_____

_____

_____

_____

_____

_____

_____

"And they overcame him because of the blood of the Lamb, and because of the word of their testimony; and they loved not their life even unto death."
Revelation 12:11 ASV

God Says: ____/____/____

_____

_____

_____

_____

_____

_____

_____

_____

_____

_____

_____

_____

_____

_____

_____

_____

_____

_____

"Their destiny is destruction, their god is their stomach, and their glory is in their shame. Their mind is set on earthly things."
Philippians 3:19 NIV

God Says: _____/_____/_____

_____

_____

_____

_____

_____

_____

_____

_____

_____

_____

_____

_____

_____

_____

_____

_____

_____

_____

_____

"Understand this, my dear brothers and sisters: You must all be quick to listen, slow to speak, and slow to get angry. Human anger does not produce the righteousness God desires."
James 1:19-20 NLT

God Says: _____/_____/_____

_____

_____

_____

_____

_____

_____

_____

_____

_____

_____

_____

_____

_____

_____

_____

_____

_____

_____

"But as for me, I watch in hope for the Lord, I wait for God my Savior; my God will hear me."
Micah 7:7 NIV

God Says: _____ / _____ / _____

_____

_____

_____

_____

_____

_____

_____

_____

_____

_____

_____

_____

_____

_____

_____

_____

_____

_____

_____

"God is our refuge and strength, A very present help in trouble."
Psalm 46:1 KJV

God Says: _____/_____/_____

"Who among you fears the Lord and obeys the word of his servant? Let the one who walks in the dark, who has no light, trust in the name of the Lord and rely on their God."
Isaiah 50:10 NIV

God Says: _____/_____/_____

_____

_____

_____

_____

_____

_____

_____

_____

_____

_____

_____

_____

_____

_____

_____

_____

_____

_____

_____

"Adulterers and adulteresses! Do you not know that friendship with the world is enmity with God? Whoever therefore wants to be a friend of the world makes himself an enemy of God."
James 4:4 NKJV

God Says: _____/_____/_____

_____

_____

_____

_____

_____

_____

_____

_____

_____

_____

_____

_____

_____

_____

_____

_____

_____

_____

"Then shall thy light break forth as the morning, and thine health shall spring forth speedily: and thy righteousness shall go before thee; the glory of the LORD shall be thy rereward."
Isaiah 58:8 KJV

God Says: _____ / _____ / _____

_____

_____

_____

_____

_____

_____

_____

_____

_____

_____

_____

_____

_____

_____

_____

_____

_____

_____

"And he answered, Fear not: for they that be with us are more than they that be with them. And Elisha prayed, and said, LORD, I pray thee, open his eyes, that he may see. And the LORD opened the eyes of the young man; and he saw: and, behold, the mountain was full of horses and chariots of fire round about Elisha." 2 Kings 6:16-17 KJV

God Says: _____/_____/_____

_____

_____

_____

_____

_____

_____

_____

_____

_____

_____

_____

_____

_____

_____

_____

_____

_____

_____

"I praise you because I am fearfully and wonderfully made; your works are wonderful, I know that full well." Psalms 139:14 NIV

God Says: _____/_____/_____

_____

_____

_____

_____

_____

_____

_____

_____

_____

_____

_____

_____

_____

_____

_____

_____

_____

"My people are destroyed for lack of knowledge. Because you have rejected knowledge, I also will reject you from being priest for Me; Because you have forgotten the law of your God, I also will forget your children." Hosea 4:6 NKJV

God Says: _____/_____/_____

_____

_____

_____

_____

_____

_____

_____

_____

_____

_____

_____

_____

_____

_____

_____

_____

_____

_____

"For he shall give his angels charge over thee, To keep thee in all thy ways. They shall bear thee up in their hands, Lest thou dash thy foot against a stone."
Psalm 91:11-12 KJV

God Says: _____/_____/_____

_____

_____

_____

_____

_____

_____

_____

_____

_____

_____

_____

_____

_____

_____

_____

_____

_____

_____

_____

"But be ye doers of the word, and not hearers only, deceiving your own selves."
James 1:22 KJV

God Says: _____/_____/_____

_____

_____

_____

_____

_____

_____

_____

_____

_____

_____

_____

_____

_____

_____

_____

_____

_____

"For this reason God highly exalted Him and gave Him the name that is above every name, so that at the name of Jesus every knee will bow—of those who are in heaven and on earth and under the earth—and every tongue should confess that Jesus Christ is Lord, to the glory of God the Father."
Philippians 2:9-11 HCSB

God Says: _____/_____/_____

_____

_____

_____

_____

_____

_____

_____

_____

_____

_____

_____

_____

_____

_____

_____

_____

_____

_____

"And the LORD shall help them, and deliver them: He shall deliver them from the wicked, and save them, because they trust in him."
Psalm 37:40 KJV

God Says: _____/_____/_____

_____

_____

_____

_____

_____

_____

_____

_____

_____

_____

_____

_____

_____

_____

_____

_____

_____

_____

"The one who follows instruction is on the path to life, but the one who rejects correction goes astray." Proverbs 10:17 HCSB

God Says: _____/_____/_____

_____

_____

_____

_____

_____

_____

_____

_____

_____

_____

_____

_____

_____

_____

_____

_____

_____

_____

"The heart is deceitful above all things and beyond cure. Who can understand it?"
Jeremiah 17:9 NIV

God Says: _____/_____/_____

_____

_____

_____

_____

_____

_____

_____

_____

_____

_____

_____

_____

_____

_____

_____

_____

_____

_____

"Then you call on the name of your god, and I will call on the name of the Lord. The god who answers by fire—he is God." Then all the people said, "What you say is good.""
1 Kings 18:24 NIV

God Says: _____/_____/_____

_____

_____

_____

_____

_____

_____

_____

_____

_____

_____

_____

_____

_____

_____

_____

_____

_____

_____

_____

"The Spirit of God, who raised Jesus from the dead, lives in you. And just as God raised Christ Jesus from the dead, he will give life to your mortal bodies by this same Spirit living within you." Romans 8:11 NLT

God Says: _____/_____/_____

_____

_____

_____

_____

_____

_____

_____

_____

_____

_____

_____

_____

_____

_____

_____

_____

_____

_____

"And if ye walk contrary unto me, and will not hearken unto me; I will bring seven times more plagues upon you according to your sins."
Leviticus 26:21 KJV

God Says: _____ / _____ / _____

_____

_____

_____

_____

_____

_____

_____

_____

_____

_____

_____

_____

_____

_____

_____

_____

_____

"The name of the LORD is a strong tower: The righteous runneth into it, and is safe."
Proverbs 18:10 KJV

God Says: _____/_____/_____

_____

_____

_____

_____

_____

_____

_____

_____

_____

_____

_____

_____

_____

_____

_____

_____

_____

"Samuel was displeased with their request and went to the Lord for guidance. "Do everything they say to you," the Lord replied, "for they are rejecting me, not you. They don't want me to be their king any longer." 1 Samuel 8:6-7 NLT

God Says: _____/_____/_____

_____

_____

_____

_____

_____

_____

_____

_____

_____

_____

_____

_____

_____

_____

_____

_____

_____

_____

_____

"Submit yourselves therefore to God. Resist the devil, and he will flee from you. Draw nigh to God, and he will draw nigh to you. Cleanse your hands, ye sinners; and purify your hearts, ye double minded." James 4:7-8 KJV

God Says: _____/_____/_____

_____

_____

_____

_____

_____

_____

_____

_____

_____

_____

_____

_____

_____

_____

_____

_____

_____

_____

"You prepare a table before me in the presence of my enemies. You anoint my head with oil; my cup overflows." Psalms 23:5 NIV

God Says: _____ / _____ / _____

_____

_____

_____

_____

_____

_____

_____

_____

_____

_____

_____

_____

_____

_____

_____

_____

_____

_____

_____

_____

_____

"Don't forget to show hospitality to strangers, for some who have done this have entertained angels without realizing it!" Hebrews 13:2 NLT

God Says: _____/_____/_____

_____

_____

_____

_____

_____

_____

_____

_____

_____

_____

_____

_____

_____

_____

_____

_____

_____

_____

_____

"But now the LORD my God hath given me rest on every side, so that there is neither adversary nor evil occurrent." 1 Kings KJV

God Says: _____/_____/_____

_____

_____

_____

_____

_____

_____

_____

_____

_____

_____

_____

_____

_____

_____

_____

_____

_____

_____

_____

_____

"Bless the LORD, ye his angels, that excel in strength, That do his commandments, hearkening unto the voice of his word." Psalm 103:20 KJV

God Says: _____/_____/_____

_____

_____

_____

_____

_____

_____

_____

_____

_____

_____

_____

_____

_____

_____

_____

_____

_____

_____

_____

"Preach the word; be prepared in season and out of season; correct, rebuke and encourage—with great patience and careful instruction."
2 Timothy 4:2 NIV

God Says: _____/_____/_____

_____

_____

_____

_____

_____

_____

_____

_____

_____

_____

_____

_____

_____

_____

_____

_____

_____

_____

_____

_____

"O taste and see that the LORD is good: Blessed is the man that trusteth in him."
Psalm 34:8 KJV

God Says: _____/_____/_____

_____

_____

_____

_____

_____

_____

_____

_____

_____

_____

_____

_____

_____

_____

_____

_____

_____

"I will worship toward thy holy temple, and praise thy name for thy lovingkindness and for thy truth: For thou hast magnified thy word above all thy name."
Psalm 138:2 KJV

God Says:

_____/_____/_____

"Every good and perfect gift is from above, coming down from the Father of the heavenly lights, who does not change like shifting shadows."

James 1:17 NIV

God Says: _____/_____/_____

_____

_____

_____

_____

_____

_____

_____

_____

_____

_____

_____

_____

_____

_____

_____

_____

_____

_____

"Then if my people who are called by my name will humble themselves and pray and seek my face and turn from their wicked ways, I will hear from heaven and will forgive their sins and restore their land." 2 Chronicles 7:14 NLT

God Says: _____/_____/_____

_____

_____

_____

_____

_____

_____

_____

_____

_____

_____

_____

_____

_____

_____

_____

_____

_____

_____

_____

_____

"I searched for a man among them who would repair the wall and stand in the gap before Me on behalf of the land so that I might not destroy it, but I found no one."
Ezekiel 22:30 HCSB

God Says: _____ / _____ / _____

_____

_____

_____

_____

_____

_____

_____

_____

_____

_____

_____

_____

_____

_____

_____

_____

_____

_____

"I sought the Lord, and He heard me, And delivered me from all my fears. They looked to Him and were radiant, And their faces were not ashamed."
Psalms 34:4-5 NKJV

God Says: _____/_____/_____

_____

_____

_____

_____

_____

_____

_____

_____

_____

_____

_____

_____

_____

_____

_____

_____

_____

_____

"For I am the Lord your God who takes hold of your right hand and says to you, Do not fear; I will help you." Isaiah 41:13 NIV

God Says: _____/_____/_____

_____

_____

_____

_____

_____

_____

_____

_____

_____

_____

_____

_____

_____

_____

_____

_____

_____

_____

"But Jesus turning and seeing her said, Daughter, be of good cheer; thy faith hath made thee whole. And the woman was made whole from that hour."
Matthew 9:22 ASV

God Says: _____/_____/_____

"Our soul waiteth for the LORD: He is our help and our shield."
Psalm 33:20 KJV

God Says: _____/_____/_____

_____

_____

_____

_____

_____

_____

_____

_____

_____

_____

_____

_____

_____

_____

_____

_____

_____

_____

_____

"I have been young, and now am old; Yet have I not seen the righteous forsaken, nor his seed begging bread." Psalm 37:25 KJV

God Says: _____/_____/_____

_____

_____

_____

_____

_____

_____

_____

_____

_____

_____

_____

_____

_____

_____

_____

_____

_____

_____

"not looking to your own interests but each of you to the interests of the others."
Philippians 2:4 NIV

God Says: _____/_____/_____

_____

_____

_____

_____

_____

_____

_____

_____

_____

_____

_____

_____

_____

_____

_____

_____

_____

_____

_____

"So they rose early in the morning and went out into the Wilderness of Tekoa; and as they went out, Jehoshaphat stood and said, "Hear me, O Judah and you inhabitants of Jerusalem: Believe in the Lord your God, and you shall be established; believe His prophets, and you shall prosper.""
II Chronicles 20:20 NKJV

God Says:

_____ / _____ / _____

_____

_____

_____

_____

_____

_____

_____

_____

_____

_____

_____

_____

_____

_____

_____

_____

_____

_____

_____

_____

_____

"Sow to yourselves in righteousness, reap in mercy; break up your fallow ground: for it is time to seek the LORD, till he come and rain righteousness upon you."

Hosea 10:12 KJV

God Says: _____ / _____ / _____

_____

_____

_____

_____

_____

_____

_____

_____

_____

_____

_____

_____

_____

_____

_____

_____

_____

_____

"The fear of the LORD prolongeth days: But the years of the wicked shall be shortened."
Proverbs 10:27 KJV

God Says: _____ / _____ / _____

_____

_____

_____

_____

_____

_____

_____

_____

_____

_____

_____

_____

_____

_____

_____

_____

_____

_____

"I will go before you And make the crooked places straight; I will break in pieces the gates of bronze And cut the bars of iron."

Isaiah 45:2 NKJV

God Says: _____/_____/_____

_____

_____

_____

_____

_____

_____

_____

_____

_____

_____

_____

_____

_____

_____

_____

_____

_____

_____

"Hope deferred makes the heart sick, But when the desire comes, it is a tree of life."
Proverbs 13:12 NKJV

God Says: _____ / _____ / _____

_____

_____

_____

_____

_____

_____

_____

_____

_____

_____

_____

_____

_____

_____

_____

_____

_____

_____

"An excellent wife is the crown of her husband, But she who causes shame is like rottenness in his bones." Proverbs 12:4 NKJV

God Says: _____/_____/_____

_____

_____

_____

_____

_____

_____

_____

_____

_____

_____

_____

_____

_____

_____

_____

_____

_____

_____

"Do not forget to entertain strangers, for by so doing some have unwittingly entertained angels."
Hebrews 13:2 NKJV

God Says: _____/_____/_____

_____

_____

_____

_____

_____

_____

_____

_____

_____

_____

_____

_____

_____

_____

_____

_____

_____

_____

_____

_____

"That they may know from the rising of the sun to its setting That there is none besides Me. I am the Lord, and there is no other; I form the light and create darkness, I make peace and create calamity; I, the Lord, do all these things." Isaiah 45:6-7 NKJV

God Says: _____/_____/_____

_____

_____

_____

_____

_____

_____

_____

_____

_____

_____

_____

_____

_____

_____

_____

_____

_____

"Kind words are like honey— sweet to the soul and healthy for the body."
Proverbs 16:24 NLT

God Says: _____ / _____ / _____

_____

_____

_____

_____

_____

_____

_____

_____

_____

_____

_____

_____

_____

_____

_____

_____

_____

_____

_____

_____

_____

"Let us not become weary in doing good, for at the proper time we will reap a harvest if we do not give up." Galatians 6:9 NIV

God Says: _____/_____/_____

_____

_____

_____

_____

_____

_____

_____

_____

_____

_____

_____

_____

_____

_____

_____

_____

_____

_____

_____

"Ask the Lord your God for a sign, whether in the deepest depths or in the highest heights."
Isaiah 7:11 NIV

God Says: _____/_____/_____

_____

_____

_____

_____

_____

_____

_____

_____

_____

_____

_____

_____

_____

_____

_____

_____

_____

_____

_____

"And from the days of John the Baptist until now the kingdom of heaven suffers violence, and the violent take it by force." Matthew 11:12 NKJV

God Says: _____/_____/_____

_____

_____

_____

_____

_____

_____

_____

_____

_____

_____

_____

_____

_____

_____

_____

_____

_____

_____

"Dear friends, do not believe every spirit, but test the spirits to see whether they are from God, because many false prophets have gone out into the world."
1 John 4:1 NIV

God Says: _____ / _____ / _____

_____

_____

_____

_____

_____

_____

_____

_____

_____

_____

_____

_____

_____

_____

_____

_____

_____

"Consider the work of God; For who can make straight what He has made crooked? In the day of prosperity be joyful, But in the day of adversity consider: Surely God has appointed the one as well as the other, So that man can find out nothing that will come after him."
Ecclesiastes 7:13-14 NKJV

God Says: _____/_____/_____

_____

_____

_____

_____

_____

_____

_____

_____

_____

_____

_____

_____

_____

_____

_____

_____

_____

_____

_____

_____

_____

"Then I heard a loud voice saying in heaven, "Now salvation, and strength, and the kingdom of our God, and the power of His Christ have come, for the accuser of our brethren, who accused them before our God day and night, has been cast down. And they overcame him by the blood of the Lamb and by the word of their testimony, and they did not love their lives to the death."" Revelation 12:10-11 NKJV

God Says: _____ / _____ / _____

_____

_____

_____

_____

_____

_____

_____

_____

_____

_____

_____

_____

_____

_____

_____

_____

_____

_____

"The Lord confides in those who fear him; he makes his covenant known to them."
Psalms 25:14 NIV

God Says: _____/_____/_____

_____

_____

_____

_____

_____

_____

_____

_____

_____

_____

_____

_____

_____

_____

_____

_____

_____

"And all the people who were at the gate, and the elders, said, "We are witnesses. The Lord make the woman who is coming to your house like Rachel and Leah, the two who built the house of Israel; and may you prosper in Ephrathah and be famous in Bethlehem."" Ruth 4:11 NKJV

God Says: _____/_____/_____

_____

_____

_____

_____

_____

_____

_____

_____

_____

_____

_____

_____

_____

_____

_____

_____

_____

"And he said, "Listen, all you of Judah and you inhabitants of Jerusalem, and you, King Jehoshaphat! Thus says the Lord to you: Do not be afraid nor dismayed because of this great multitude, for the battle is not yours, but God's."" II Chronicles 20:15 NKJV

God Says: _____/_____/_____

_____

_____

_____

_____

_____

_____

_____

_____

_____

_____

_____

_____

_____

_____

_____

_____

_____

_____

"The Lord bless you and keep you; The Lord make His face shine upon you, And be gracious to you; The Lord lift up His countenance upon you, And give you peace." Numbers 6:24-26 NKJV

God Says: _____/_____/_____

_____

_____

_____

_____

_____

_____

_____

_____

_____

_____

_____

_____

_____

_____

_____

_____

_____

_____

_____

"But the God of all grace, who hath called us unto his eternal glory by Christ Jesus, after that ye have suffered a while, make you perfect, stablish, strengthen, settle you." 1 Peter 5:10 KJV

God Says: _____/_____/_____

_____

_____

_____

_____

_____

_____

_____

_____

_____

_____

_____

_____

_____

_____

_____

_____

_____

_____

_____

"Behold, the days come, saith the LORD, that I will perform that good thing which I have promised unto the house of Israel and to the house of Judah." Jeremiah 33:14 KJV

God Says: _____ / _____ / _____

_____

_____

_____

_____

_____

_____

_____

_____

_____

_____

_____

_____

_____

_____

_____

_____

_____

_____

"And he believed in the LORD; and He counted it to him for righteousness."

Genesis 15:6 KJV

God Says: _____/_____/_____

_____

_____

_____

_____

_____

_____

_____

_____

_____

_____

_____

_____

_____

_____

_____

_____

_____

_____

_____

_____

"Blessed is the man that trusteth in the Lord, and whose hope the LORD is."

Jeremiah 17:7 KJV

God Says: _____/_____/_____

_____

_____

_____

_____

_____

_____

_____

_____

_____

_____

_____

_____

_____

_____

_____

_____

_____

_____

"and whenever you turn to the right or to the left, your ears will hear this command behind you: "This is the way. Walk in it."" Isaiah 30:21 HCSB

God Says: _____/_____/_____

_____

_____

_____

_____

_____

_____

_____

_____

_____

_____

_____

_____

_____

_____

_____

"Now the Spirit of the Lord had left Saul, and an evil spirit sent from the Lord began to torment him," 1 Samuel 16:14 HCSB

God Says: _____ / _____ / _____

_____

_____

_____

_____

_____

_____

_____

_____

_____

_____

_____

_____

_____

_____

_____

_____

_____

_____

_____

_____

_____

"For it is not an enemy who reproaches me; Then I could bear it. Nor is it one who hates me who has exalted himself against me; Then I could hide from him. But it was you, a man my equal, My companion and my acquaintance. We took sweet counsel together, And walked to the house of God in the throng."
Psalms 55:12-14 NKJV

God Says: _____/_____/_____

_____

_____

_____

_____

_____

_____

_____

_____

_____

_____

_____

_____

_____

_____

_____

_____

_____

"Surely He has borne our griefs And carried our sorrows; Yet we esteemed Him stricken, Smitten by God, and afflicted. But He was wounded for our transgressions, He was bruised for our iniquities; The chastisement for our peace was upon Him, And by His stripes we are healed."
Isaiah 53:4-5 NKJV

God Says: _____/_____/_____

_____

_____

_____

_____

_____

_____

_____

_____

_____

_____

_____

_____

_____

_____

_____

_____

_____

_____

"But Ruth replied, "Don't urge me to leave you or to turn back from you. Where you go I will go, and where you stay I will stay. Your people will be my people and your God my God. Where you die I will die, and there I will be buried. May the Lord deal with me, be it ever so severely, if even death separates you and me."" Ruth 1:16-17 NIV

God Says: _____/_____/_____

_____

_____

_____

_____

_____

_____

_____

_____

_____

_____

_____

_____

_____

_____

_____

_____

_____

_____

"The young lions do lack, and suffer hunger: But they that seek the LORD shall not want any good thing." Psalm 34:10 KJV

God Says: _____ / _____ / _____

_____

_____

_____

_____

_____

_____

_____

_____

_____

_____

_____

_____

_____

_____

_____

_____

_____

_____

_____

_____

_____

"May the grace of the Lord Jesus Christ be with your spirit."
Philemon 1:25 NLT

God Says:

_____/_____/_____

_____

_____

_____

_____

_____

_____

_____

_____

_____

_____

_____

_____

_____

_____

_____

_____

"But the fruit of the Spirit is love, joy, peace, patience, kindness, goodness, faith, gentleness, self-control. Against such things there is no law."
Galatians 5:22-23 HCSB

God Says: _____/_____/_____

_____

_____

_____

_____

_____

_____

_____

_____

_____

_____

_____

_____

_____

_____

_____

_____

_____

_____

_____

_____

"Do not remember the former things, Nor consider the things of old. Behold, I will do a new thing, Now it shall spring forth; Shall you not know it? I will even make a road in the wilderness And rivers in the desert." Isaiah 43:18-19 NKJV

God Says: _____/_____/_____

_____

_____

_____

_____

_____

_____

_____

_____

_____

_____

_____

_____

_____

_____

_____

_____

_____

_____

_____

"The lion hath roared, who will not fear? The Lord GOD hath spoken, who can but prophesy?"
Amos 3:8 KJV

God Says: ＿＿＿ / ＿＿＿ / ＿＿＿

＿＿＿＿＿＿＿＿＿＿＿＿＿＿＿＿＿＿＿＿＿＿＿＿＿＿

＿＿＿＿＿＿＿＿＿＿＿＿＿＿＿＿＿＿＿＿＿＿＿＿＿＿

＿＿＿＿＿＿＿＿＿＿＿＿＿＿＿＿＿＿＿＿＿＿＿＿＿＿

＿＿＿＿＿＿＿＿＿＿＿＿＿＿＿＿＿＿＿＿＿＿＿＿＿＿

＿＿＿＿＿＿＿＿＿＿＿＿＿＿＿＿＿＿＿＿＿＿＿＿＿＿

＿＿＿＿＿＿＿＿＿＿＿＿＿＿＿＿＿＿＿＿＿＿＿＿＿＿

＿＿＿＿＿＿＿＿＿＿＿＿＿＿＿＿＿＿＿＿＿＿＿＿＿＿

＿＿＿＿＿＿＿＿＿＿＿＿＿＿＿＿＿＿＿＿＿＿＿＿＿＿

＿＿＿＿＿＿＿＿＿＿＿＿＿＿＿＿＿＿＿＿＿＿＿＿＿＿

＿＿＿＿＿＿＿＿＿＿＿＿＿＿＿＿＿＿＿＿＿＿＿＿＿＿

＿＿＿＿＿＿＿＿＿＿＿＿＿＿＿＿＿＿＿＿＿＿＿＿＿＿

＿＿＿＿＿＿＿＿＿＿＿＿＿＿＿＿＿＿＿＿＿＿＿＿＿＿

＿＿＿＿＿＿＿＿＿＿＿＿＿＿＿＿＿＿＿＿＿＿＿＿＿＿

＿＿＿＿＿＿＿＿＿＿＿＿＿＿＿＿＿＿＿＿＿＿＿＿＿＿

＿＿＿＿＿＿＿＿＿＿＿＿＿＿＿＿＿＿＿＿＿＿＿＿＿＿

＿＿＿＿＿＿＿＿＿＿＿＿＿＿＿＿＿＿＿＿＿＿＿＿＿＿

＿＿＿＿＿＿＿＿＿＿＿＿＿＿＿＿＿＿＿＿＿＿＿＿＿＿

"The Lord helps them and delivers them; he delivers them from the wicked and saves them, because they take refuge in him."

Psalms 37:40 NIV

God Says:

_____/_____/_____

_____

_____

_____

_____

_____

_____

_____

_____

_____

_____

_____

_____

_____

_____

_____

_____

_____

"Do not be afraid; you will not be put to shame. Do not fear disgrace; you will not be humiliated. You will forget the shame of your youth and remember no more the reproach of your widowhood." Isaiah 54:4 NIV

God Says: _____/_____/_____

_____

_____

_____

_____

_____

_____

_____

_____

_____

_____

_____

_____

_____

_____

_____

_____

_____

_____

_____

"Restore the joy of Your salvation to me, and give me a willing spirit."
Psalms 51:12 HCSB

God Says: _____ / _____ / _____

_____

_____

_____

_____

_____

_____

_____

_____

_____

_____

_____

_____

_____

_____

_____

_____

_____

_____

"It shall come to pass in that day That his burden will be taken away from your shoulder, And his yoke from your neck, And the yoke will be destroyed because of the anointing oil."
Isaiah 10:27 NKJV

God Says: _____/_____/_____

_____

_____

_____

_____

_____

_____

_____

_____

_____

_____

_____

_____

_____

_____

_____

_____

_____

_____

"Then King David went in and sat before the Lord; and he said: "Who am I, O Lord God? And what is my house, that You have brought me this far?."" I Chronicles 17:16 NKJV

God Says: _____/_____/_____

_____

_____

_____

_____

_____

_____

_____

_____

_____

_____

_____

_____

_____

_____

_____

_____

_____

"And yet this was a small thing in Your sight, O God; and You have also spoken of Your servant's house for a great while to come, and have regarded me according to the rank of a man of high degree, O Lord God." I Chronicles 17:17 NKJV

God Says: _____/_____/_____

_____

_____

_____

_____

_____

_____

_____

_____

_____

_____

_____

_____

_____

_____

_____

_____

_____

"You shall no longer be termed Forsaken, Nor shall your land any more be termed Desolate; But you shall be called Hephzibah, and your land Beulah; For the Lord delights in you, And your land shall be married." 62:4 NKJV

God Says: 			_____/_____/_____

_____

_____

_____

_____

_____

_____

_____

_____

_____

_____

_____

_____

_____

_____

_____

_____

_____

"Elijah went before the people and said, "How long will you waver between two opinions? If the Lord is God, follow him; but if Baal is God, follow him." But the people said nothing."

1 Kings 18:21 NIV

God Says: _____ / _____ / _____

_____

_____

_____

_____

_____

_____

_____

_____

_____

_____

_____

_____

_____

_____

_____

_____

_____

_____

_____

_____

_____

"and give him no rest, till he establish, and till he make Jerusalem a praise in the earth."
Isaiah 62:7 KJV

God Says: _____/_____/_____

_____

_____

_____

_____

_____

_____

_____

_____

_____

_____

_____

_____

_____

_____

_____

_____

_____

_____

"But now your kingdom will not endure; the Lord has sought out a man after his own heart and appointed him ruler of his people, because you have not kept the Lord's command."
1 Samuel 13:14 NIV

God Says: _____/_____/_____

_____

_____

_____

_____

_____

_____

_____

_____

_____

_____

_____

_____

_____

_____

_____

_____

_____

_____

_____

"Death and life are in the power of the tongue: And they that love it shall eat the fruit thereof."
Proverbs 18:21 KJV

God Says: _____/_____/_____

_____

_____

_____

_____

_____

_____

_____

_____

_____

_____

_____

_____

_____

_____

_____

_____

_____

_____

_____

"And ye shall seek me, and find me, when ye shall search for me with all your heart."
Jeremiah 29:13 KJV

God Says: _____ / _____ / _____

_____

_____

_____

_____

_____

_____

_____

_____

_____

_____

_____

_____

_____

_____

_____

_____

_____

_____

"Then touched he their eyes, saying, According to your faith be it unto you."
Matthew 9:29 KJV

God Says: _____/_____/_____

_____

_____

_____

_____

_____

_____

_____

_____

_____

_____

_____

_____

_____

_____

_____

_____

_____

"Am I now trying to win the approval of human beings, or of God? Or am I trying to please people? If I were still trying to please people, I would not be a servant of Christ."
Galatians 1:10 NIV

God Says: _____/_____/_____

_____

_____

_____

_____

_____

_____

_____

_____

_____

_____

_____

_____

_____

_____

_____

_____

_____

_____

"Yes, and from ancient days I am he. No one can deliver out of my hand. When I act, who can reverse it?" Isaiah 43:13 NIV

God Says: _____/_____/_____

_____

_____

_____

_____

_____

_____

_____

_____

_____

_____

_____

_____

_____

_____

_____

_____

_____

"The Angel of the Lord encamps around those who fear Him, and rescues them."
Psalms 34:7 HCSB

God Says: _____/_____/_____

_____

_____

_____

_____

_____

_____

_____

_____

_____

_____

_____

_____

_____

_____

_____

_____

_____

_____

_____

"And the Lord said, "Simon, Simon! Indeed, Satan has asked for you, that he may sift you as wheat. But I have prayed for you, that your faith should not fail; and when you have returned to Me, strengthen your brethren."" Luke 22:31-32 NKJV

God Says: _____/_____/_____

_____

_____

_____

_____

_____

_____

_____

_____

_____

_____

_____

_____

_____

_____

_____

_____

_____

_____

_____

"Do all things without complaining and disputing, that you may become blameless and harmless, children of God without fault in the midst of a crooked and perverse generation, among whom you shine as lights in the world," Philippians 2:14-15 NKJV

God Says: _____ / _____ / _____

_____

_____

_____

_____

_____

_____

_____

_____

_____

_____

_____

_____

_____

_____

_____

_____

_____

_____

"Where no counsel is, the people fall: But in the multitude of counselors there is safety."
Proverbs 11:14 KJV

God Says: ____ / ____ / ____

_____

_____

_____

_____

_____

_____

_____

_____

_____

_____

_____

_____

_____

_____

_____

_____

_____

_____

"But the Counselor, the Holy Spirit — the Father will send Him in My name — will teach you
all things and remind you of everything I have told you."
John 14:26 HCSB

God Says: _____/_____/_____

_____

_____

_____

_____

_____

_____

_____

_____

_____

_____

_____

_____

_____

_____

_____

_____

_____

_____

_____

_____

"For the time will come when people will not put up with sound doctrine. Instead, to suit their own desires, they will gather around them a great number of teachers to say what their itching ears want to hear." 2 Timothy 4:3 NIV

God Says: _____/_____/_____

_____

_____

_____

_____

_____

_____

_____

_____

_____

_____

_____

_____

_____

_____

_____

_____

_____

_____

_____

"They will turn their ears away from the truth and turn aside to myths. But you, keep your head in all situations, endure hardship, do the work of an evangelist, discharge all the duties of your ministry." 2 Timothy 4:4-5 NIV

God Says: _____/_____/_____

_____

_____

_____

_____

_____

_____

_____

_____

_____

_____

_____

_____

_____

_____

_____

_____

_____

_____

_____

_____

"In thee, O LORD, do I put my trust; Let me never be ashamed: deliver me in thy righteousness. Bow down thine ear to me; deliver me speedily: Be thou my strong rock, for an house of defense to save me."
Psalm 31:1-2 KJV

God Says: _____ / _____ / _____

_____

_____

_____

_____

_____

_____

_____

_____

_____

_____

_____

_____

_____

_____

_____

_____

"Peace I leave with you, my peace I give unto you: not as the world giveth, give I unto you. Let not your heart be troubled, neither let it be afraid."

John 14:27 KJV

God Says:

_____/_____/_____

"If ye shall ask any thing in my name, I will do it."
John 14:14 KJV

God Says: _____/_____/_____

_____

_____

_____

_____

_____

_____

_____

_____

_____

_____

_____

_____

_____

_____

_____

_____

_____

_____

"But David said to Abishai, "Don't destroy him! Who can lay a hand on the Lord's anointed and be guiltless?"" 1 Samuel 26:9 NIV

God Says: _____/_____/_____

_____

_____

_____

_____

_____

_____

_____

_____

_____

_____

_____

_____

_____

_____

_____

_____

_____

_____

_____

_____

_____

_____

"Take delight in the Lord, and he will give you the desires of your heart."
Psalms 37:4 NIV

God Says: _____/_____/_____

_____

_____

_____

_____

_____

_____

_____

_____

_____

_____

_____

_____

_____

_____

_____

_____

_____

_____

"To humans belong the plans of the heart, but from the Lord comes the proper answer of the tongue. All a person's ways seem pure to them, but motives are weighed by the Lord. Commit to the Lord whatever you do, and he will establish your plans. The Lord works out everything to its proper end— even the wicked for a day of disaster." Proverbs 16:1-4 NIV

God Says: _____ / _____ / _____

_____

_____

_____

_____

_____

_____

_____

_____

_____

_____

_____

_____

_____

_____

_____

_____

_____

_____

_____

_____

"He who finds a wife finds a good thing, And obtains favor from the Lord."
Proverbs 18:22 NKJV

God Says: _____/_____/_____

_____

_____

_____

_____

_____

_____

_____

_____

_____

_____

_____

_____

_____

_____

_____

_____

_____

""As for me," God says, "this is my covenant with them: My Spirit that I've placed upon you and the words that I've given you to speak, they're not going to leave your mouths nor the mouths of your children nor the mouths of your grandchildren. You will keep repeating these words and won't ever stop." God's orders."" Isaiah 59:21 MSG

God Says: _____/_____/_____

_____

_____

_____

_____

_____

_____

_____

_____

_____

_____

_____

_____

_____

_____

_____

_____

_____

_____

"This is what the Lord says: If you can break my covenant with the day and the night so that one does not follow the other, only then will my covenant with my servant David be broken. Only then will he no longer have a descendant to reign on his throne. The same is true for my covenant with the Levitical priests who minister before me." Jeremiah 33:20-21 NLT

God Says: _____/_____/_____

_____

_____

_____

_____

_____

_____

_____

_____

_____

_____

_____

_____

_____

_____

_____

_____

_____

_____

_____

"I have declared the former things from of old; yea, they went forth out of my mouth, and I showed them: suddenly I did them, and they came to pass." Isaiah 48:3 ASV

God Says:

_____/_____/_____

_____

_____

_____

_____

_____

_____

_____

_____

_____

_____

_____

_____

_____

_____

_____

_____

_____

_____

_____

_____

"God is not a man, that he should lie; Neither the son of man, that he should repent: Hath he said, and shall he not do it? Or hath he spoken, and shall he not make it good? Behold, I have received commandment to bless: And he hath blessed; and I cannot reverse it." Numbers 23:19-20 KJV

God Says: _____/_____/_____

_____

_____

_____

_____

_____

_____

_____

_____

_____

_____

_____

_____

_____

_____

_____

_____

_____

_____

"Then he answered and spake unto me, saying, This is the word of the LORD unto Zerubbabel, saying, Not by might, nor by power, but by my spirit, saith the LORD of hosts." Zechariah 4:6 KJV

God Says: _____/_____/_____

_____

_____

_____

_____

_____

_____

_____

_____

_____

_____

_____

_____

_____

_____

_____

_____

_____

_____

"For we were saved in this hope, but hope that is seen is not hope; for why does one still hope for what he sees? But if we hope for what we do not see, we eagerly wait for it with perseverance."
Romans 8:24-25 NKJV

God Says: _____/_____/_____

_____

_____

_____

_____

_____

_____

_____

_____

_____

_____

_____

_____

_____

_____

_____

_____

_____

_____

"But He gives greater grace. Therefore He says: God resists the proud, but gives grace to the humble." James 4:6 HCSB

God Says: _____/_____/_____

_____

_____

_____

_____

_____

_____

_____

_____

_____

_____

_____

_____

_____

_____

_____

_____

_____

_____

_____

_____

_____

_____

"A thousand may fall at your side, ten thousand at your right hand, but it will not come near you." Psalms 91:7 NIV

God Says: _____ / _____ / _____

_____

_____

_____

_____

_____

_____

_____

_____

_____

_____

_____

_____

_____

_____

_____

_____

_____

_____

_____

_____

_____

"The Lord is near to those who have a broken heart, And saves such as have a contrite spirit."
Psalms 34:18 NKJV

God Says: ____/____/____

_____

_____

_____

_____

_____

_____

_____

_____

_____

_____

_____

_____

_____

_____

_____

_____

_____

"He is near who justifies Me; Who will contend with Me? Let us stand together. Who is My adversary? Let him come near Me."
Isaiah 50:8 NKJV

God Says: _____/_____/_____

_____

_____

_____

_____

_____

_____

_____

_____

_____

_____

_____

_____

_____

_____

_____

_____

_____

"But the Lord said to me, "Do not say, 'I am too young.' You must go to everyone I send you to and say whatever I command you.""
Jeremiah 1:7 NIV

God Says: _____/_____/_____

_____

_____

_____

_____

_____

_____

_____

_____

_____

_____

_____

_____

_____

_____

_____

_____

_____

_____

_____

_____

"For with the heart one believes unto righteousness, and with the mouth confession is made unto salvation. For the Scripture says, "Whoever believes on Him will not be put to shame." For "whoever calls on the name of the Lord shall be saved.""
Romans 10:10-11, 13 NKJV

God Says: _____/_____/_____

_____

_____

_____

_____

_____

_____

_____

_____

_____

_____

_____

_____

_____

_____

_____

_____

_____

"For My name's sake I will defer My anger, And for My praise I will restrain it from you, So that I do not cut you off. Behold, I have refined you, but not as silver; I have tested you in the furnace of affliction. For My own sake, for My own sake, I will do it; For how should My name be profaned? And I will not give My glory to another." Isaiah 48:9-11 NKJV

God Says: _____/_____/_____

_____

_____

_____

_____

_____

_____

_____

_____

_____

_____

_____

_____

_____

_____

_____

_____

_____

_____

_____

"Then Eliezer son of Dodavahu from Mareshah prophesied against Jehoshaphat." He said, "Because you have allied yourself with King Ahaziah, the Lord will destroy your work." So the ships met with disaster and never put out to sea." 2 Chronicles 20:37 NLT

God Says: _____ / _____ / _____

_____

_____

_____

_____

_____

_____

_____

_____

_____

_____

_____

_____

_____

_____

_____

_____

_____

"Pride goes before destruction, And a haughty spirit before a fall."
Proverbs 16:18 NKJV

God Says: ____ / ____ / ____

_____

_____

_____

_____

_____

_____

_____

_____

_____

_____

_____

_____

_____

_____

_____

_____

_____

_____

_____

_____

"I waited patiently for the LORD; And he inclined unto me, and heard my cry. He brought me up also out of an horrible pit, out of the miry clay, And set my feet upon a rock, and established my goings. And he hath put a new song in my mouth, even praise unto our God: Many shall see it, and fear, And shall trust in the LORD." Psalm 40:1-3 KJV

God Says: _____/_____/_____

_____

_____

_____

_____

_____

_____

_____

_____

_____

_____

_____

_____

_____

_____

_____

_____

_____

_____

_____

_____

"In their hearts humans plan their course, but the Lord establishes their steps."
Proverbs 16:9 NIV

God Says: _____/_____/_____

_____

_____

_____

_____

_____

_____

_____

_____

_____

_____

_____

_____

_____

_____

_____

_____

_____

_____

_____

_____

_____

"For no matter how many promises God has made, they are "Yes" in Christ. And so through him the "Amen" is spoken by us to the glory of God." 2 Corinthians 1:20 NIV

God Says: _____/_____/_____

_____

_____

_____

_____

_____

_____

_____

_____

_____

_____

_____

_____

_____

_____

_____

_____

_____

"When tempted, no one should say, "God is tempting me." For God cannot be tempted by evil, nor does he tempt anyone; but each person is tempted when they are dragged away by their own evil desire and enticed. Then, after desire has conceived, it gives birth to sin; and sin, when it is full-grown, gives birth to death. Don't be deceived, my dear brothers and sisters." James 1:13-16 NIV

God Says: _____/_____/_____

_____

_____

_____

_____

_____

_____

_____

_____

_____

_____

_____

_____

_____

_____

_____

_____

_____

_____

"God is within her, she will not fall; God will help her at break of day."
Psalms 46:5 NIV

God Says: _____/_____/_____

_____

_____

_____

_____

_____

_____

_____

_____

_____

_____

_____

_____

_____

_____

_____

_____

_____

"You have turned my mourning into joyful dancing. You have taken away my clothes of mourning and clothed me with joy," Psalms 30:11 NLT

God Says: _____ / _____ / _____

_____

_____

_____

_____

_____

_____

_____

_____

_____

_____

_____

_____

_____

_____

_____

_____

_____

_____

_____

_____

_____

"Because the Sovereign Lord helps me, I will not be disgraced. Therefore have I set my face like flint, and I know I will not be put to shame." Isaiah 50:7 NIV

God Says: _____/_____/_____

_____

_____

_____

_____

_____

_____

_____

_____

_____

_____

_____

_____

_____

_____

_____

_____

_____

"Get yourself ready! Stand up and say to them whatever I command you. Do not be terrified by them, or I will terrify you before them."
Jeremiah 1:17 NIV

God Says: _____/_____/_____

_____

_____

_____

_____

_____

_____

_____

_____

_____

_____

_____

_____

_____

_____

_____

_____

_____

_____

_____

_____

"Get yourself ready! Stand up and say to them whatever I command you. Do not be terrified by them, or I will terrify you before them."
Jeremiah 1:17 NIV

God Says: _____/_____/_____

_____

_____

_____

_____

_____

_____

_____

_____

_____

_____

_____

_____

_____

_____

_____

_____

_____

_____

"But the Advocate, the Holy Spirit, whom the Father will send in my name, will teach you all
things and will remind you of everything I have said to you."
John 14:26 NIV

God Says: _____/_____/_____

_____

_____

_____

_____

_____

_____

_____

_____

_____

_____

_____

_____

_____

_____

_____

_____

_____

_____

"Blessed is he who considers the poor; The Lord will deliver him in time of trouble. The Lord will preserve him and keep him alive, And he will be blessed on the earth; You will not deliver him to the will of his enemies. The Lord will strengthen him on his bed of illness; You will sustain him on his sickbed. I said, "Lord, be merciful to me; Heal my soul, for I have sinned against You."" Psalms 41:1-4 NKJV

God Says: _____/_____/_____

_____

_____

_____

_____

_____

_____

_____

_____

_____

_____

_____

_____

_____

_____

_____

_____

_____

"Very truly I tell you, unless a kernel of wheat falls to the ground and dies, it remains only a single seed. But if it dies, it produces many seeds."
John 12:24 NIV

God Says: _____ / _____ / _____

_____

_____

_____

_____

_____

_____

_____

_____

_____

_____

_____

_____

_____

_____

_____

_____

_____

_____

_____

"Wash away my guilt and cleanse me from my sin. For I am conscious of my rebellion, and my sin is always before me. Against You — You alone — I have sinned and done this evil in Your sight. So You are right when You pass sentence; You are blameless when You judge."
Psalms 51:2-4 HCSB

God Says: _____/_____/_____

_____

_____

_____

_____

_____

_____

_____

_____

_____

_____

_____

_____

_____

_____

_____

_____

_____

_____

"And they blessed Rebekah and said to her, "Our sister, may you increase to thousands upon thousands; may your offspring possess the cities of their enemies.""
Genesis 24:60 NIV

God Says: _____/_____/_____

_____

_____

_____

_____

_____

_____

_____

_____

_____

_____

_____

_____

_____

_____

_____

_____

_____

_____

_____

_____

"Blessed is the one who trusts in the Lord, who does not look to the proud, to those who turn aside to false gods." Psalms 40:4 NIV

God Says: _____/_____/_____

_____

_____

_____

_____

_____

_____

_____

_____

_____

_____

_____

_____

_____

_____

_____

_____

_____

_____

_____

"When a man's ways please the Lord, He makes even his enemies to be at peace with him."
Proverbs 16:7 NKJV

God Says: ____/____/____

_____

_____

_____

_____

_____

_____

_____

_____

_____

_____

_____

_____

_____

_____

_____

_____

_____

"but the Lord laughs at the wicked, for he knows their day is coming."
Psalms 37:13 NIV

God Says:

_____/_____/_____

""Yes indeed, it won't be long now." God's Decree. "Things are going to happen so fast your head will swim, one thing fast on the heels of the other. You won't be able to keep up. Everything will be happening at once—and everywhere you look, blessings! Blessings like wine pouring off the mountains and hills.." Amos 9:13 MSG

God Says:

_____ / _____ / _____

God Says: _____/_____/_____

_____

_____

_____

_____

_____

_____

_____

_____

_____

_____

_____

_____

_____

_____

_____

_____

_____

_____

_____

"Unless the Lord builds the house, They labor in vain who build it; Unless the Lord guards the city, The watchman stays awake in vain. It is vain for you to rise up early, To sit up late, To eat the bread of sorrows; For so He gives His beloved sleep." Psalms 127:1-2 NKJV

God Says: _____/_____/_____

_____

_____

_____

_____

_____

_____

_____

_____

_____

_____

_____

_____

_____

_____

_____

_____

_____

_____

_____

_____

"thus saith the Lord GOD, It shall not stand, neither shall it come to pass."
Isaiah 7:7 KJV

God Says: _____/_____/_____

_____

_____

_____

_____

_____

_____

_____

_____

_____

_____

_____

_____

_____

_____

_____

_____

_____

_____

"And, behold, thy cousin Elisabeth, she hath also conceived a son in her old age: and this is the sixth month with her, who was called barren. For with God nothing shall be impossible."
Luke 1:36-37 KJV

God Says: ____ / ____ / ____

_____

_____

_____

_____

_____

_____

_____

_____

_____

_____

_____

_____

_____

_____

_____

_____

_____

_____

_____

_____

_____

""I also tell you this: If two of you agree here on earth concerning anything you ask, my Father in heaven will do it for you. For where two or three gather together as my followers, I am there among them."" Matthew 18:19-20 NLT

God Says: ____/____/____

_____

_____

_____

_____

_____

_____

_____

_____

_____

_____

_____

_____

_____

_____

_____

_____

_____

_____

_____

""For My thoughts are not your thoughts, Nor are your ways My ways," says the Lord. "For as the heavens are higher than the earth, So are My ways higher than your ways, And My thoughts than your thoughts." Isaiah 55:8-9 NKJV

God Says: _____/_____/_____

_____

_____

_____

_____

_____

_____

_____

_____

_____

_____

_____

_____

_____

_____

_____

_____

_____

"For as the rain comes down, and the snow from heaven, And do not return there, But water the earth, And make it bring forth and bud, That it may give seed to the sower And bread to the eater,"

Isaiah 55:10 NKJV

God Says: _____/_____/_____

_____

_____

_____

_____

_____

_____

_____

_____

_____

_____

_____

_____

_____

_____

_____

_____

_____

_____

"So shall My word be that goes forth from My mouth; It shall not return to Me void, But it shall accomplish what I please, And it shall prosper in the thing for which I sent it." Isaiah 55:11 NKJV

God Says: _____/_____/_____

_____

_____

_____

_____

_____

_____

_____

_____

_____

_____

_____

_____

_____

_____

_____

_____

_____

_____

"The world would love you as one of its own if you belonged to it, but you are no longer part of the world. I chose you to come out of the world, so it hates you."

John 15:19 NLT

God Says: _____ / _____ / _____

_____

_____

_____

_____

_____

_____

_____

_____

_____

_____

_____

_____

_____

_____

_____

_____

_____

_____

"Let all things be done decently and in order."
I Corinthians 14:40 NKJV

God Says: _____/_____/_____

_____

_____

_____

_____

_____

_____

_____

_____

_____

_____

_____

_____

_____

_____

_____

_____

_____

"Then Nathan said to David, "Do all that is in your heart, for God is with you.""
I Chronicles 17:2 NKJV

God Says: _____/_____/_____

_____

_____

_____

_____

_____

_____

_____

_____

_____

_____

_____

_____

_____

_____

_____

_____

_____

_____

"So I will restore to you the years that the swarming locust has eaten, The crawling locust, The consuming locust, And the chewing locust, My great army which I sent among you."
Joel 2:25 NKJV

God Says: _____/_____/_____

_____

_____

_____

_____

_____

_____

_____

_____

_____

_____

_____

_____

_____

_____

_____

_____

_____

_____

_____

"See, I have this day set you over the nations and over the kingdoms, To root out and to pull down, To destroy and to throw down, To build and to plant."
Jeremiah 1:10 NKJV

God Says: _____/_____/_____

_____

_____

_____

_____

_____

_____

_____

_____

_____

_____

_____

_____

_____

_____

_____

_____

_____

_____

"With long life I will satisfy him, And show him My salvation."
Psalms 91:16 NKJV

God Says: _____/_____/_____

_____

_____

_____

_____

_____

_____

_____

_____

_____

_____

_____

_____

_____

_____

_____

_____

_____

_____

"Where can I go from Your Spirit? Or where can I flee from Your presence? If I ascend into heaven, You are there; If I make my bed in hell, behold, You are there."
Psalms 139:7-8 NKJV

God Says: _____/_____/_____

_____

_____

_____

_____

_____

_____

_____

_____

_____

_____

_____

_____

_____

_____

_____

_____

_____

"Many are the afflictions of the righteous, But the Lord delivers him out of them all."
Psalms 34:19 NKJV

God Says: _____/_____/_____

_____

_____

_____

_____

_____

_____

_____

_____

_____

_____

_____

_____

_____

_____

_____

_____

_____

_____

_____

_____

"And be not conformed to this world: but be ye transformed by the renewing of your mind, that ye may prove what is that good, and acceptable, and perfect, will of God."
Romans 12:2 KJV

God Says: _____/_____/_____

_____

_____

_____

_____

_____

_____

_____

_____

_____

_____

_____

_____

_____

_____

_____

_____

_____

""Today I have made you a fortified city, an iron pillar and a bronze wall to stand against the whole land—against the kings of Judah, its officials, its priests and the people of the land. They will fight against you but will not overcome you, for I am with you and will rescue you," declares the Lord." Jeremiah 1:18-19 NIV

God Says: _____/_____/_____

_____

_____

_____

_____

_____

_____

_____

_____

_____

_____

_____

_____

_____

_____

_____

_____

_____

_____

_____

_____

"And you shall remember the Lord your God, for it is He who gives you power to get wealth, that He may establish His covenant which He swore to your fathers, as it is this day."
Deuteronomy 8:18 NKJV

God Says: _____/_____/_____

_____

_____

_____

_____

_____

_____

_____

_____

_____

_____

_____

_____

_____

_____

_____

_____

_____

_____

_____

_____

"And we know that all things work together for good to those who love God, to those who are the called according to His purpose." Romans 8:28 NKJV

God Says: _____ / _____ / _____

_____

_____

_____

_____

_____

_____

_____

_____

_____

_____

_____

_____

_____

_____

_____

_____

_____

_____

_____

_____

"But even the very hairs of your head are all numbered. Fear not therefore: ye are of more value than many sparrows." Luke 12:7 KJV

God Says: _____/_____/_____

_____

_____

_____

_____

_____

_____

_____

_____

_____

_____

_____

_____

_____

_____

_____

_____

_____

"Trust in the Lord with all your heart, And lean not on your own understanding; In all your ways acknowledge Him, And He shall direct your paths."
Proverbs 3:5-6 NKJV

God Says: _____/_____/_____

_____

_____

_____

_____

_____

_____

_____

_____

_____

_____

_____

_____

_____

_____

_____

_____

_____

_____

_____

_____

_____

_____

"And He called the twelve to Himself, and began to send them out two by two, and gave them power over unclean spirits." Mark 6:7 NKJV

God Says: _____/_____/_____

_____

_____

_____

_____

_____

_____

_____

_____

_____

_____

_____

_____

_____

_____

_____

_____

_____

_____

_____

“The LORD will perfect that which concerneth me: Thy mercy, O LORD, endureth for ever:
Forsake not the works of thine own hands.”
Psalm 138:8 KJV

God Says: _____ / _____ / _____

_____

_____

_____

_____

_____

_____

_____

_____

_____

_____

_____

_____

_____

_____

_____

_____

_____

_____

_____

_____

"For wisdom is a defense, and money is a defense: but the excellency of knowledge is, that wisdom giveth life to them that have it."

Ecclesiastes 7:12 KJV

God Says: _____/_____/_____

_____

_____

_____

_____

_____

_____

_____

_____

_____

_____

_____

_____

_____

_____

_____

_____

_____

_____

"And it came to pass, when he had made an end of speaking unto Saul, that the soul of Jonathan was knit with the soul of David, and Jonathan loved him as his own soul."

1 Samuel 18:1 KJV

God Says: _____/_____/_____

"Who shall ascend into the hill of the LORD? Or who shall stand in his holy place? He that hath clean hands, and a pure heart; Who hath not lifted up his soul unto vanity, nor sworn deceitfully."

Psalm 24:3-4 KJV

God Says: _____/_____/_____

_____

_____

_____

_____

_____

_____

_____

_____

_____

_____

_____

_____

_____

_____

_____

_____

_____

_____

_____

_____

_____

"Before I formed you in the womb I knew you, before you were born I set you apart; I appointed you as a prophet to the nations." Jeremiah 1:5 NIV

God Says: _____ / _____ / _____

_____

_____

_____

_____

_____

_____

_____

_____

_____

_____

_____

_____

_____

_____

_____

_____

_____

"For whom he did foreknow, he also did predestinate to be conformed to the image of his Son, that he might be the firstborn among many brethren. Moreover whom he did predestinate, them he also called: and whom he called, them he also justified: and whom he justified, them he also glorified."
Romans 8:29-30 KJV

God Says: _____/_____/_____

_____

_____

_____

_____

_____

_____

_____

_____

_____

_____

_____

_____

_____

_____

_____

_____

_____

""How foolish!" Samuel exclaimed. "You have not kept the command the Lord your God gave you. Had you kept it, the Lord would have established your kingdom over Israel forever.""
1 Samuel 13:13 NLT

God Says: _____/_____/_____

_____

_____

_____

_____

_____

_____

_____

_____

_____

_____

_____

_____

_____

_____

_____

_____

_____

_____

_____

"But now your kingdom must end, for the Lord has sought out a man after his own heart. The Lord has already appointed him to be the leader of his people, because you have not kept the Lord's command." 1 Samuel 13:14 NLT

God Says: _____/_____/_____

_____

_____

_____

_____

_____

_____

_____

_____

_____

_____

_____

_____

_____

_____

_____

_____

_____

_____

"God, create a clean heart for me and renew a steadfast spirit within me."
Psalms 51:10 HCSB

God Says: _____/_____/_____

_____

_____

_____

_____

_____

_____

_____

_____

_____

_____

_____

_____

_____

_____

_____

_____

_____

"Lazy hands make for poverty, but diligent hands bring wealth." Proverbs 10:4 NIV

God Says: _____/_____/_____

_____

_____

_____

_____

_____

_____

_____

_____

_____

_____

_____

_____

_____

_____

_____

_____

_____

_____

"I will give you the treasures of darkness And hidden riches of secret places, That you may know that I, the Lord, Who call you by your name, Am the God of Israel." Isaiah 45:3 NKJV

God Says: _____ / _____ / _____

_____

_____

_____

_____

_____

_____

_____

_____

_____

_____

_____

_____

_____

_____

_____

_____

_____

_____

_____

"Then an angel appeared to Him from heaven, strengthening Him. And being in agony, He prayed more earnestly. Then His sweat became like great drops of blood falling down to the ground." Luke 22:43-44 NKJV

God Says: _____/_____/_____

_____

_____

_____

_____

_____

_____

_____

_____

_____

_____

_____

_____

_____

_____

_____

_____

_____

_____

"Ye shall not fear them: for the LORD your God he shall fight for you."
Deuteronomy 3:22 KJV

God Says: _____/_____/_____

_____

_____

_____

_____

_____

_____

_____

_____

_____

_____

_____

_____

_____

_____

_____

_____

_____

_____

_____

"For I am persuaded that neither death nor life, nor angels nor principalities nor powers, nor things present nor things to come, nor height nor depth, nor any other created thing, shall be able to separate us from the love of God which is in Christ Jesus our Lord." Romans 8:35 & 37 NKJV

God Says: _____/_____/_____

_____

_____

_____

_____

_____

_____

_____

_____

_____

_____

_____

_____

_____

_____

_____

_____

_____

_____

"for you are a people holy to the Lord your God. Out of all the peoples on the face of the earth, the Lord has chosen you to be his treasured possession."

Deuteronomy 14:2 NIV

God Says: _____/_____/_____

_____

_____

_____

_____

_____

_____

_____

_____

_____

_____

_____

_____

_____

_____

_____

_____

_____

_____

"You have recorded my troubles. You have kept a list of my tears. Aren't they in your records?"
Psalms 56:8 ICB

God Says: _____/_____/_____

_____

_____

_____

_____

_____

_____

_____

_____

_____

_____

_____

_____

_____

_____

_____

_____

_____

_____

"My brethren, count it all joy when you fall into various trials, knowing that the testing of your faith produces patience. But let patience have its perfect work, that you may be perfect and complete, lacking nothing." James 1:2-8 NKJV

God Says: _____/_____/_____

_____

_____

_____

_____

_____

_____

_____

_____

_____

_____

_____

_____

_____

_____

_____

_____

_____

_____

"If any of you lacks wisdom, let him ask of God, who gives to all liberally and without reproach, and it will be given to him. But let him ask in faith, with no doubting, for he who doubts is like a wave of the sea driven and tossed by the wind. For let not that man suppose that he will receive anything from the Lord; he is a double-minded man, unstable in all his ways." James 1:2-8 NKJV

God Says:

_____/_____/_____

_____

_____

_____

_____

_____

_____

_____

_____

_____

_____

_____

_____

_____

_____

_____

_____

_____

"For God hath not given us the spirit of fear; but of power, and of love, and of a sound mind."
2 Timothy 1:7 KJV

God Says: _____/_____/_____

_____

_____

_____

_____

_____

_____

_____

_____

_____

_____

_____

_____

_____

_____

_____

_____

_____

_____

"Thus saith the LORD, thy Redeemer, the Holy One of Israel; I am the LORD thy God which teacheth thee to profit, which leadeth thee by the way that thou shouldest go." Isaiah 48:17 KJV

God Says: _____/_____/_____

_____

_____

_____

_____

_____

_____

_____

_____

_____

_____

_____

_____

_____

_____

_____

_____

_____

_____

_____

_____

"If you help the poor, you are lending to the Lord— and he will repay you!"
Proverbs 19:17 NLT

God Says: _____/_____/_____

_____

_____

_____

_____

_____

_____

_____

_____

_____

_____

_____

_____

_____

_____

_____

_____

_____

_____

_____

"What shall we then say to these things? If God be for us, who can be against us?"
Romans 8:31 KJV

God Says: _____/_____/_____

_____

_____

_____

_____

_____

_____

_____

_____

_____

_____

_____

_____

_____

_____

_____

_____

_____

_____

"The LORD is my light and my salvation; whom shall I fear? The LORD is the strength of my life; of whom shall I be afraid?" Psalm 27:1 KJV

God Says:

_____/_____/_____

_____

_____

_____

_____

_____

_____

_____

_____

_____

_____

_____

_____

_____

_____

_____

_____

_____

_____

_____

"For I know the plans I have for you," declares the Lord, "plans to prosper you and not to harm you, plans to give you hope and a future."" Jeremiah 29:11 NIV

God Says: _____/_____/_____

_____

_____

_____

_____

_____

_____

_____

_____

_____

_____

_____

_____

_____

_____

_____

_____

_____

_____

_____

"But you are a chosen people, a royal priesthood, a holy nation, God's special possession, that
you may declare the praises of him who called you out of darkness into his wonderful light."
1 Peter 2:9 NIV

God Says: _____ / _____ / _____

_____

_____

_____

_____

_____

_____

_____

_____

_____

_____

_____

_____

_____

_____

_____

_____

_____

_____

_____

_____

"Who will bring any charge against those whom God has chosen? It is God who justifies."
Romans 8:33 NIV

God Says: _____/_____/_____

_____

_____

_____

_____

_____

_____

_____

_____

_____

_____

_____

_____

_____

_____

_____

_____

_____

_____

"If ye abide in me, and my words abide in you, ye shall ask what ye will, and it shall be done unto you." John 15:7 KJV

God Says: _____/_____/_____

_____

_____

_____

_____

_____

_____

_____

_____

_____

_____

_____

_____

_____

_____

_____

_____

_____

_____

"And He said to me, "My grace is sufficient for you, for My strength is made perfect in weakness." Therefore most gladly I will rather boast in my infirmities, that the power of Christ may rest upon me. Therefore I take pleasure in infirmities, in reproaches, in needs, in persecutions, in distresses, for Christ's sake. For when I am weak, then I am strong." II Corinthians 12:9-10 NKJV

God Says: _____ / _____ / _____

_____

_____

_____

_____

_____

_____

_____

_____

_____

_____

_____

_____

_____

_____

_____

_____

_____

_____

"Then you will call on me and come and pray to me, and I will listen to you. You will seek me and find me when you seek me with all your heart."
Jeremiah 29:12-13 NIV

God Says: _____/_____/_____

_____

_____

_____

_____

_____

_____

_____

_____

_____

_____

_____

_____

_____

_____

_____

_____

_____

_____

_____

_____

"For I am persuaded that neither death nor life, nor angels nor principalities nor powers, nor things present nor things to come, nor height nor depth, nor any other created thing, shall be able to separate us from the love of God which is in Christ Jesus our Lord." Romans 8:38-39 NKJV

God Says: _____/_____/_____

_____

_____

_____

_____

_____

_____

_____

_____

_____

_____

_____

_____

_____

_____

_____

_____

_____

_____

"You, indeed, have made my days short in length, and my life span as nothing in Your sight. Yes, every mortal man is only a vapor." _Selah_ Psalms 39:5 HCSB

God Says: _____/_____/_____

_____

_____

_____

_____

_____

_____

_____

_____

_____

_____

_____

_____

_____

_____

_____

_____

_____

"'But if they confess their iniquity and the iniquity of their fathers, with their unfaithfulness in which they were unfaithful to Me, and that they also have walked contrary to Me, and that I also have walked contrary to them and have brought them into the land of their enemies; if their uncircumcised hearts are humbled, and they accept their guilt." Leviticus 26:40-41 NKJV

God Says: _____/_____/_____

_____

_____

_____

_____

_____

_____

_____

_____

_____

_____

_____

_____

_____

_____

_____

_____

_____

_____

"Then I will remember My covenant with Jacob, and My covenant with Isaac and My covenant with Abraham I will remember; I will remember the land." Leviticus 26:42 NKJV

God Says: _____/_____/_____

_____

_____

_____

_____

_____

_____

_____

_____

_____

_____

_____

_____

_____

_____

_____

_____

_____

_____

_____

_____

_____

"Ask thee a sign of the LORD thy God; ask it either in the depth, or in the height above."
Isaiah 7:11 KJV

God Says: _____/_____/_____

_____

_____

_____

_____

_____

_____

_____

_____

_____

_____

_____

_____

_____

_____

_____

_____

_____

_____

"Lift up your heads, O you gates! And be lifted up, you everlasting doors! And the King of glory shall come in. Who is this King of glory? The Lord strong and mighty, The Lord mighty in battle. Lift up your heads, O you gates! Lift up, you everlasting doors! And the King of glory shall come in. Who is this King of glory? The Lord of hosts, He is the King of glory." _Selah_ Psalms 24:7-10 NKJV

Start by identifying which curses and patterns from the verses in Deuteronomy 28:15-68 that plague you and your bloodline. Ask God to replace the curses from Deut. 28:15-68 with the blessings of Deut. 28:1-14. Also, ask Holy Spirit to reveal what brought these covenants and curses into your life and on your bloodline (idolatry, service to another god, etc.), this way you can experience true repentance and never fall back into the same curses and covenants again.

1. **Repent.** "God, forgive me for all my sins, iniquities, and transgressions. I am deeply sorry for what I have done that has displeased you. If there are sins, iniquities, and transgressions I have done that I don't know about or remember, bring them to mind so I won't do them again; I want true repentance. I am agreeing with my adversary [satan] quickly, whatever the adversary says I have done, I take off the spirit of pride and agree, forgive me, God. Through my repentance, I break legal rights, it will no longer speak against me. I also repent for my bloodline according to Leviticus 26:40-42. God put me and my bloodline in remembrance."

2. **Renounce/Come out of agreement.** "God, I renounce, denounce and come out of agreement with every evil covenant made on any evil altar that has been made through my family's or my own sins, iniquities, and transgressions."

3. **Replace.** Ask God to replace whatever is happening with healing according to the stripes Jesus took on the cross (Isaiah 53:5-6). (Find the opposite of what's happening and speak the opposite or the antonym of what you're experiencing). E.g. replace generational poverty with generational wealth. Replace the sicknesses, diseases, early death, etc. with long life and good health. Replace the generational curses with generational blessings (Matthew 12:43-45). "God, as I call for the replacing of these curses, help me to also remember that faith without works is dead. I speak these prayers by faith, but teach me how to also work with Holy Spirit to do what it is you desire to see done in my life and bloodline, in the name of Jesus, amen."

4. **Rule, Reign, Dominion.** "God, I have repented, renounced, and replaced these curses that have appeared in my life as a result of evil covenants made by me or someone in my bloodline. Because you are a God of grace, please give me and my bloodline a holy and legal pardon in the realm of the spirit, instead of consequences. Pardon me so I don't reap the evil harvest of what was done. I speak the remission of sins over evil covenants and curses. God, I give you rule, reign, and dominion over me and my bloodline. Exonerate us. God, have your way."

5. **Rebuke satan.** James 4:7 says, "Therefore submit to God. Resist the devil and he will flee from you." Matthew 4:10 says, "Then Jesus said to him, "Away with you, Satan! For it is written, 'You shall worship the Lord your God, and Him only you shall serve.'"

"Satan, you are now rebuked and I command you to flee from my life and my family's life. You have no access to attack us in this area. As we stay in a repentant heart posture, should you try and attack in this area, you are in high treason. I decree and declare no trace or residue of any curse will be on my life or my bloodline. I declare, me and my family are whole and healed. We will live and not die to declare the works of the Lord.

6. **Bonus.** Please Note* Some curses can be broken from simple identification & repentance, while some curses are stubborn and generational, they have been on a bloodline for ages and won't come out unless through prayer and biblical fasting (no food, only water for a period of time designated to you by God). This is according to Matthew 17:21 "This 'kind' won't come out unless through prayer and fasting." (Kind=*genos*, kindred, offspring, nation, family, stock, tribe, race, etc..).

God Says Journal
Copyright © 2023 by Kayla Fointno
All rights reserved.

Published By: Books By KJF Self-Publishing, LLC

ISBN: 979-8-9897684-0-0

Contributors:

Scripture quotations marked MSG are taken from *THE MESSAGE*, copyright © 1993, 2002, 2018 by Eugene H. Peterson. Used by permission of NavPress. All rights reserved. Represented by Tyndale House Publishers, Inc.

Scripture quotations marked (NLT) are taken from the *Holy Bible*, New Living Translation, copyright ©1996, 2004, 2015 by Tyndale House Foundation. Used by permission of Tyndale House Publishers, Carol Stream, Illinois 60188. All rights reserved.

THE HOLY BIBLE, NEW INTERNATIONAL VERSION®, NIV® Copyright © 1973, 1978, 1984, 2011 by Biblica, Inc.® Used by permission. All rights reserved worldwide.

Scripture quotations marked HCSB are taken from the Holman Christian Standard Bible®, Copyright © 1999, 2000, 2002, 2003, 2009 by Holman Bible Publishers. Used by permission. Holman Christian Standard Bible®, Holman CSB®, and HCSB® are federally registered trademarks of Holman Bible Publishers.

Scriptures quoted from the International Children's Bible®, copyright ©1986, 1988, 1999, 2015 by Tommy Nelson. Used by permission.

Scripture taken from the New King James Version®. Copyright © 1982 by Thomas Nelson. Used by permission. All rights reserved.

Also used: King James Version which is public domain.

Also used: American Standard Version which is public domain.

BOOKS BY KJF
Self-Publishing
"Everyone has a book on the inside of them waiting to be discovered."